The Practice of Hypnosis & Hypnotherapy

An Anthology of Articles

2011 Edition

Compiled by
Michael Scott &
The Editors at
Blue Deck Press

Portions of this work have been previously published on the internet sites HypnosisArticlesDirectory.com and CreeksideHypnosis.com and are published pursuant to the grants of authority from those organizations.

The Practice of Hypnosis and Hypnotherapy, 2011 Edition
Copyright 2011 - Michael S. Spillan
All Rights Reserved

Preface

The use of hypnosis as a form of therapy goes back to the dawn of history. Only in the last 150 years, though, has it been approached as a science, and only in the last 75 years has Western society begun looking at hypnotherapy as the legitimate healing tool it can be and is.

In the United States, and elsewhere, hypnotherapy is practiced not so much by psychiatrists and psychologists as it is by holistic and "alternative" practitioners. There are no national standards for hypnotherapy. There are several reputable organizations, and at least one nationally accredited college of hypnotherapy, all contributing to the growth and increasing credibility of this important field.

For the new practitioner (and the experienced one as well) there are few comprehensive sources of guidance on the establishment and growth of a solid and ethical practice.

The Practice of Hypnosis is an anthology of articles, by contemporary practitioners, most of which have been previously published elsewhere. Included are articles on hypnosis and Neuro-Linguistic Programming (NLP), opening and maintaining a practice, use of scripts, self-hypnosis, the growing field of erotic hypnosis and numerous other areas, each carefully screened from a list of hundreds of submissions.

Several of the articles in this work are written by authors in the United Kingdom (as many of the subtle languages differences will attest) where the practice of hypnosis seems to be coming to the mainstream faster than it has in the United States.

Many of the articles here were originally commercial advertising pieces, but all of them contain information which can be helpful to the experienced and beginning practitioner.

Each of these articles is available for reprint without additional release, as long as they are reprinted in their entirety, author credits and resources included, and are printed herein individually to assist in copying for those who may desire to do so.

It is my hope to watch the practice continue to grow more commonplace and to gain greater acceptance in the coming years and decades, and it is my wish that this work, to be revised regularly, will contribute in some small way to that growth.

This work is dedicated to the three most important women in my life. To my Mother, Jane Spillan, who has always encouraged to grow and learn, to my wonderful wife, Melissa, who adds beauty and wonder to my world in such endless supply that I sometimes think I am in the presence of a goddess, and to Miranda who makes me laugh and smile with the most outrageous questions and ideas and who, with Mom and Missy, manages to round out the beautiful things in my life nicely.

As always, I am open to ideas and suggestions, comments criticisms and, should you be literarily inclined, articles for possible inclusions in future editions[1].

Mike Scott Spillan
November 11, 2010
Columbus, Ohio

---

[1] Please send any correspondence to: mike.scott@bluedeckpress.com

With great love and adoration, this book is dedicated to my wife Melissa, who encourages me to learn, even when distracted by other things, to share, when I would withdraw, and to grow, even in the hardest of times and environments.

Table of Contents

Section I   **The Basics of Hypnosis**

        Nam et ipsa scientia potestas es

Section II   **Neuro-Linguistic Programming**

        Libenter homines id quod volunt credunt

Section III   **The Practice of Hypnotherapy (In Office and Remote)**

        Numquam aliud natura, aliud sapientia dicit

Section IV   **Treatment - The Invocation of Change**

        Transire suum pectus mundoque potiri

Section V   **Resources**

        Sit vis vobiscum - May the Force be with you. (Star Wars)

Section VI   **Laws, Forms, Suggestions and More**

        Magnus frater spectat te - Big Brother is watching you

Article and Author Index

Section I

The Basics of Hypnosis

Nam et ipsa scientia potestas es
"Knowledge is power" (Sir Francis Bacon)

Treating Your Tools with Respect

or

Everything I Ever Needed to Know About Hypnosis
I Learned in High School

by

Michael S. Spillan

During the waning days of summer in 1981, I sat with 30 new classmates listening to my Latin-I teacher explain why a language that fell out of popular use 1,300 years ago is relevant to me, today. I remember thinking later that it must have been the monotone quality of his voice, or maybe the odd cadence with which he spoke, but somewhere shortly into his speech I noticed that many of my compatriots were staring, glass-eyed, at Mr. Balskis while most of the rest of us were fighting hard to remain alert.

Later, in the evening, I relayed to my Father how hard I thought the class was going to be for me, not because of the subject matter, but rather because of the trouble I had staying awake with the teacher. Couldn't stay focused, I complained.

Dad, a psychiatric social worker, listened, asked a couple of questions, and pronounced, "You weren't distracted, Michael, you were paying attention, *really focused*."

Over the next half hour I got my first instruction in hypnosis, beginning a lifelong fascination with the subject. From Franz Mesmer to Milton Erickson, I found its history fascinating, and, as in most things, Dad was right: Mr. Balskis was, quite unconsciously I believe, a natural hypnotist. If he had opened an office and hung out a shingle he could have made a fortune. Luckily for me[2] and countless others, he remained a teacher.

There are countless schools of thought about how hypnosis works[3], and I will not attempt to address them all here. The articles in Section I of this book deal with how hypnotic theory and with some of what can be done with it. All of them, and the countless others I have read in preparation of this work, come from different schools of hypnosis, and all of them have something different to share. Some are short, some are long, a few are mostly advertising pieces, but all of them contain solid pieces of information anyone wanting to learn hypnosis, improve their lives, or build a practice, should have.

I would point out that despite all of the disagreement in how hypnosis works, the fact of the matter is that it does. Scientifically recognized, its benefits in the hands of a competent practitioner are unquestionable. In the hands of someone who is not as competent, however, hypnosis can be as dangerous as a loaded gun in the hands of drunken child.[4]

---

[2] Said ironically, I am not, nor was I ever, much of a Latin scholar, despite my tendency to trouble others with Latin quotes.

[3] You will find mine in the article *Focus and Memory*, starting on the next page.

[4] See: *Realities and Warnings* one the last page of this work.

The Hippocratic Oath[5] admonishes medical practitioners to, first and foremost, do no harm, that is to not make things worse in trying to perfect a cure for their patients. In the practice of hypnotherapy the need for this approach cannot be stressed enough. The potential for even accidental harm cannot be understated. Even Erickson made (and to our benefit wrote about) his share of mistakes. I encourage you, whether you are reading this to learn to improve your own life, or to learn to help others, to always remember that hypnosis is a *powerful* tool and it[6] needs to be treated with the utmost respect at all times.

Remember the book *Everything I Ever Needed To Know I Learned In Kindergarten* by Robert Fulghum ? In it he explained that all of the important things about human relationships are taught at an early age: Saying "please" and "thank you", keeping your hands to yourself and leaving others' property alone. Yep, kindergarten.

In high school we learn something different, there we are taught (hopefully) how to behave toward others and the world at large. Respect for yourself, service to others, social responsibility and the need for a life spent learning, all of these are lessons of high school and they are the things we need to know about the practice of hypnosis, as well. Couple a person with no respect for these things with a little hypnotic skill and you have the recipe for disaster, keep them in mind and a person should do very well.

---

[5] Every version of it back to the Latin version: *Primum non nocere* - "The first thing is to do no harm".

[6] Like your client, whether the client is yourself or someone else.

Hypnosis - Focus and Memory
A New Approach To Healing

by

Michael S. Spillan

Recently, I had the opportunity to again review the works of Milton Ericskon, MD, widely regarded to be the father of modern hypnotherapy, and without a doubt one of the most intuitive psychiatrists of our age.

Dr. Erickson made some of the greatest advances in hypnosis and hypnotherapy, and nearly single-handedly brought it from the fringes of recognized psychology (not to mention the backrooms stage magic) and into the realm of legitimate therapeutic sciences.

Erickson, in his written works, made little effort to quantify the science he helped to create. Instead, he shares the methods he developed and their effect. Thousands upon thousands of hours of trial and error shared generously in support of healing others.

Several scientists, most notably Ernest L. Rossi. Ph.D., have worked hard to define the bounds of Erickson's works, attempting to quantify the brilliant and intuitive efforts of a lifetime's practice into a form the rest of us are able to use to the benefit of ourselves and the people around us.

I have long admired Dr. Erickson's dedication to healing through guided hypnosis, and so it was to my collection of publications by and/or about him that I turned when I looked to answer a simple request for a plain language explanation of how hypnosis actually works.

Without meaning to disparage the two centuries of work used to develop them, common generic explanations that abound, such as

> "[Hypnosis is]..a trance state characterized by extreme suggestibility, relaxation and heightened imagination..."

can be misleading (any hypnotist knows that while relaxation is helpful in a clinical setting, it is hardly necessary) and do little to explain even the basics of how hypnosis works.

Even the recently updated definition from the Society for Psychological Hypnosis, a division of the American Psychological Association, revised in 2005[7], though long-winded (see below for the text)

---

[7]The Division 30 Definition and Description of Hypnosis:

"Hypnosis typically involves an introduction to the procedure which the subject is told that suggestions for imaginative experiences will be presented. The hypnotic induction is an extended initial suggestion for using one's says much of the induction of hypnosis and nothing of its true workings.

I am a hypnotist with a computing and engineering background. I am a tinkerer and garage scientist at heart and I simply refuse to believe that even something as complex as the workings of the human mind cannot be broken down into basic terms that anyone can understand.

For explanations of quantum physics I can follow I watch PBS, for politics I listen to talk radio[8] and for hypnosis I return to the collected works of the Master himself.

It seems to me that, based on Erickson's work (and finding nothing to the contrary, anywhere) that hypnosis, both simple and complex, works through the interplay of just two components: Focus and Memory.

Focus, in hypnosis, is simple: In a hypnotic trance the subject focuses his or her attention to the exclusion of all else. Environment, physical sensations, even self-awareness take a back seat to the item of the participant's focus. Focus in a hypnotic trance is the means by which we access the second component.

Memory, in hypnosis, is a bit more complex, but still easy to digest.

Everything we know, all of our reactions to the world, both physical and emotional, are passed through lenses colored by our life of memories.

To paraphrase, we are the sum total of our experiences.

Through the trance, the hypnotist has access to all memories, and with the consent of the subject, can change them, bringing about profound changes in the subject.

What am I talking about? Let me share a brief example:

The process of reframing is one of the most common hypnotic techniques. In reframing a hypnotist takes an undesirable reaction (say, nervousness about flying) and changes it into something more desirable (childlike excitement at trying something new).

---

imagination, and may contain further elaborations of the introduction. A hypnotic procedure is used to encourage and evaluate responses to suggestions. When using hypnosis, one person (the subject) is guided by another (the hypnotist) to respond to suggestions is changes in subjective experience, alterations in perception, sensation, emotion, thought or behavior. Persons can also learn self-hypnosis, which is the act of administering hypnotic procedures on one's own. If the subject responds to hypnotic suggestions, it is generally inferred that hypnosis has been induced. Many believe that hypnotic responses and experiences are characteristic of a hypnotic state. While some think that it is not necessary to use the word "hypnosis" as a part of hypnotic induction, others view it as essential. *"A New Definition: Hypnosis" Society of Psychological Hypnosis, Division 30 - American Psychological Association.*

[8]A vice in which I engage, but one which I do not encourage in others.

What, though, is the process? What is the hypnotist really doing? Simple: He is changing the memories linked to thinking about flying. If he is really effective and well trained, he is deliberately linking flying to recollections of excitement, fun or comfort. The hypnotist makes new memories to do this "...now see yourself walking confidently onto the plane, storing your carry-on bag in a compartment over your seat, getting into your seat. You feel good getting familiar with the seat, figuring out how the buckle works..."[9].

Little things, all plays on memory and recollection, changing how the subject perceives herself and the world around her. Even the stage cliche' "you are now a dog...a little dog, you will yip and hop and act like a dog until I tell you otherwise..." is little more than a command to "behave in the way you remember a dog would act."

In pain management (the area I first began practicing in) the most successful scripts and hypnotists change the way the body remembers reacting to pain. It is easy for a hypnotist to tell a person (your arm is numb, you can't feel it) when he really means, "no longer pay attention to your arm" (an aspect of focus), but for chronic pain control it is much better to reframe the way the body reacts to pain, changing the way it remembers reacting.

It is hard to convince the subconscious mind that it is not feeling pain that it is very much feeling. A subject can ignore it by focusing in a trance, but the pain is always there, waiting to resurface when the subject is no longer distracted.

With just a little more effort a hypnotist can change the subjects recollection of how he reacts to a particular pain, actually forming new neural pathways, turning the pain permanently into something else just a real (say tingling in their right arm or tickling down the leg)[10].

Physical and emotional changes, behavioral and perceptual, all of the things that a hypnotist may effect, through direct or indirect suggestion, are all simply influences to remember something (or the reaction to something) differently.

So, after a somewhat lengthy digression into *my* influences, let me offer this simple definition:

> "Hypnosis is an induced (or self-induced) state of extreme focus in which the person's cognitive, physical and emotional memories become accessible and highly subject to

---

[9] This is a *very* simple suggestion for example's sake.

[10] Hypnotists should *always* take care not to *eliminate* pain caused by real physical conditions. Pain exists for a reason, the subject needs to be aware that something is wrong and that, until healed, the need to be cautious exists.

suggestion or alteration."[11]

This idea has profound implications in the healing process.

Many highly effective hypnotherapists have built successful practices solely around their ability to bring about changes in their clients' cognitive memory. I wonder, though, is it not better to change how someone reacts to their painful memories (say feeling melancholy and whimsical about a painful childhood event, as opposed to feeling suppressed rage that directs itself toward his children), than it is to fiddle with the cognitive memory of the actual event, effectively denying the reality of the event?

Considering my proposed definition of hypnosis, and in light of my experience with so many of the myriad aspects hypnotherapy, I submit that healing is always best facilitated by acknowledging the truth, helping the client understand the truth, and helping them decide how they wish to react to it.

The treatment of physical discomfort can be best handled the same way.

By addressing how the body remembers the way it reacts to a particular physical sensation or pain and reinforcing the changed memory, the hypnotist can, in a lasting way, reframe that sensation or pain and better facilitate the healing process without running the extreme risks inherent in denying that the pain exists.

Agree with me or not, for those practitioners not constitutionally inclined to share my need to simplify the heretofore overly complex approaches to hypnosis that seem so characteristic of our profession, I submit that healing, in the safest, most lasting way, is the highest goal to which we can aspire as hypnotists. Something which we should all work very hard to *remember*.

---

[11] Cognitive Memory being conscious memory of circumstances and situations (e.g. recollections of your high school graduation); Physical Memory being a true physical reaction based on cognitive or emotional memory (e.g. heart racing when the commercial for that roller coaster you were on last year comes on); and, Emotional Memory being a true emotional reaction based on cognitive or physical memory (e.g. tears coming to your eyes when you think back about Uncle Jim who was always good to you).

The Handshake Interrupt And Pull Instant Hypnotic Induction

by

Nathan Thomas

If you are familiar with the traditional versions of the hypnotic handshake induction you will know that it works on the principle of pattern interrupts.

As shaking hands is something most of us just do automatically, naturally, it means it is a hard wired unconscious pattern. (like tying your shoes, writing your signature, brushing your teeth, things you just do without thinking.)

Now when this pattern is interrupted a state of total blankness is induced.

What happens is you take the mind down one track (shaking hands) which activates the unconscious pattern and automatic behavior. Just as they are comfortable on this automatic road, and their unconscious mind is operating the behavior without any conscious input you interrupt the pattern. Doing something unexpected which breaks the pattern throws their mind off the track, and leaves them in a state of total blankness, desperately searching for another track to jump on induces "hyper suggestibility." In other words, a total willingness to follow whatever you suggest (within reason of course!).

There are no limits to how you can interrupt the pattern or what pattern you can interrupt (do not restrict yourself to handshake inductions!). But in this particular induction we will focus on an arm pull.

Once you are shaking their hand and they are in the handshake pattern (just basically when they are in the act of shaking your hand in a natural and normal way) you give a sharp pull on their arm (the one you are shaking) with yours. Be sure to avoid seeming violent, and be gentle enough to ensure you do not cause any pain or injury (no folks, dislocating arms does not make a good induction!). This jerk on their arm breaks the pattern so dramatically they are hurled right off the track and enter a state of total and utter dumfoundment which you can quickly fill with your suggestion.

Now, when a clown offers his hand and then jerks it away when you go to shake it this leaves you in a dazed state for a second or so, but you soon snap out of it.
Which is why after you have broken the pattern you must act promptly to fill the gap, otherwise they will simply gather their thoughts and carry on as usual (in my experience often with total amnesia for the interrupt).

With such a dramatic break it tends to be more powerful is you are very direct and authoritarian with your suggestion.

"Sleep Now!" or just "Sleep" have proven to be very effective in my experience.

Now they're in a trance, but your work is not finished as you nearly always must then move quickly onto a deepener to ensure they stay in trance and reach an appropriate depth.

Once you have this you can give your hypnotic suggestions.

Be sure to practice this method and pattern interrupts in general to enhance your skill and confidence, and be sure to have a decent understanding of how to deepen the trance, how to give them suggestions once you have them "under," and how to emerge them once you are done.

A great learning tool is to simply have fun with it.

This method in particular may not work every time, if something does not turn out quite right treat it as a learning experience and leap back into the fray to do it again, and the more you practice the better you get, and the better you get the more fun you have!

Thanks for reading

Nathan Thomas

Author Resource:- To learn more about hypnosis and the handshake induction visit http://keystothemind.blogspot.com

PS don't forget to sign up for your free hypnotic handshake induction e-course and listen to the free hypnotic interviews and audio lessons over at http://keystothemind.blogspot.com

The Life Altering Power of Hypnosis

by

Jake Rhodes

Globally, many individuals are looking into hypnosis for a wide number of purposes. Some would like to lose weight while other people would like to ease symptoms of an illness. No matter what the motivation is, the reality is that hypnosis is certainly becoming increasingly popular. Shockingly though even many of those individuals who have experienced hypnosis do not have a great knowledge of it. So what exactly is hypnosis?

Hypnosis is a naturally occurring state of mind that the majority of people go into several times during the course of the day. The most well-known of these frequently occurring states of hypnosis is "highway hypnosis" where an individual can drive for hours in a trance, the journey seeming to fly by. TV viewing can also have a similar effect. There are various sorts of hypnosis. The couple that most people know of are stage hypnosis and hypnotherapy. Even though both types use a number of the same techniques, they do so for separate purposes. The purpose of stage hypnosis is to amuse while hypnotherapy aids people to improve their lives in a variety of ways.

Possibly because of stage hypnosis some people dismiss the values of hypnotherapy. If you've been to a stage hypnosis show you might have looked on as an audience member act as if they were glued to their chair. Some fear because of this that they will be made to do something stupid looking or manipulated in the same manner in a hypnotherapy session. This is far from the truth though. Consider this closely, in stage hypnosis the participant on stage volunteered to this performance. You cannot be hypnotized to do anything you do not want to do. Also why would a hypnotherapist carry out such a trick on a client to begin with? It is their jobs, and in their best interests, to help you successfully treat you.

When you are under hypnosis you enter a deep state of relaxation. In this state your brainwaves alter from beta to alpha. This brainwave pattern is identical as in the beginning stage of sleep. It is also thought that the hypnotic state produces theta brainwaves, and this is what opens up the unconscious mind to suggestions. You aren't in fact unconscious or asleep while under hypnosis, just deeply relaxed. You still know what is being talked about and what is happening around you.

Now we come to the vital part. How can you use hypnosis to improve your life? Well hypnosis can be used in many different ways. A variety of studies have concluded that hypnosis works well in dealing with mental, emotional and even physical problems. Most commonly individuals use hypnosis to help them with weight loss or quitting smoking but it can also be used to overcome phobias, develop better sleep patterns, increase fitness levels, accept the past and a good deal more.

There are two main options if you would like to experience hypnosis for yourself. Number one is to survey your nearby region for a hypnotherapist. You can look in your local paper in the classifieds or search online. The other choice is to go on the internet where there are many websites who employ clinical hypnotherapists to create audio recordings on various topics. This is a great starting point as CDs and MP3s are much cheaper than paying for a one to one session and can be listened to over and over again.

Author Resource:- Jake presently works at foremost hypnosis resource HypnoBusters. Visit right now to find many different hypnosis MP3s. Free hypnosis videos are also accessible on a brand new portion of the website.

Can Everyone Be Hypnotized?

by

Roseanna Leaton

This is a question which I get asked almost every day of the week. I guess being a hypnotherapist is just not a run of the mill job! Most people are more familiar with stage hypnosis than they are with its therapeutic uses and so have a fair number of questions upon the subject, including this one.

We are all unique and individual and therefore our experience of hypnosis will reflect this. Just as some people are more calm and relaxed and others more tense, and some of us are more outgoing and others more introverted, etc, some of us will enter deeper states of hypnosis than others. The depth of hypnosis reached, however, does NOT directly correspond to your normal state of calmness/tension or introversion/extraversion. In fact, hypnosis is not just a state of relaxation; it is at the same time a state of heightened awareness. And if you are anxious you will already be in a state of heightened awareness, and this can make it easier to enter hypnosis than might otherwise be the case.

In actual fact only about 5% of the population cannot be hypnotized, the rest of us will enter hypnosis to one degree or another. About 10% of people will be hypnotized very deeply, as is seen in a traditional stage show. This deep trance phenomenon is NOT needed for therapeutic purposes. ALL levels of hypnosis are conducive to therapeutic intervention.

The therapeutic applications of hypnosis are many. You may use hypnosis simply as a way to learn to totally relax and be "in the now" as you would with meditation. You can use hypnosis to aid recall, to alter habits like weight loss hypnosis or stop smoking hypnosis; you may use hypnosis to apply the principles of NLP or you may use hypnosis to dull the sensation of pain even to the extent of inducing hypno-anaesthesia.

As a hypnotherapist I am extremely lucky to have such a varied and interesting job. Hypnosis can be used to assist in anything which has a psychological aspect, which is pretty much everything. Everything which you experience in life is colored by how you think about it, by your focus, beliefs and attitudes. Hypnosis allows you to direct and control your thoughts, both conscious and subconscious, and so is a massively empowering state.

You will usually find that as you use hypnosis you will become more and more deeply hypnotizable. I recommend that anybody who is considering hypnotherapy purchases a hypnosis download, and listens to this at home a few times as an easy introduction to the natural art of hypnosis. Like most things you undertake in life, you get better at it with practice; as you use hypnosis downloads you will find that you can relax more and more deeply and quickly each time.

The hypnotic induction technique used on this type of hypnosis download is a progressive relaxation procedure. As you listen to these hypnotherapy recordings you will find that your body will become progressively more relaxed and free from tension and stress, and as this happens your mind relaxes as well. It is impossible to have a relaxed body at the same time as a tense mind, and vice versa. Hypnosis feels fantastic. It is like taking a mini holiday or giving yourself a mental massage. In this day and age there is all too much stress, tension and anxiety and so it is no wonder that so many people are turning to hypnosis downloads for help.

Reverting to the question of whether or not everyone is hypnotizable, the answer is yes, so long as you can attend to and understand the spoken word, and so long as you WANT to. And who would not want to benefit from the therapeutic power of this normal and natural state?

Roseanna Leaton, specialist in hypnosis downloads for health, self-improvement, well-being and success.

Author Resource:- With a degree in psychology and qualifications in hypnotherapy, NLP and sports psychology, Roseanna Leaton is one of the leading practitioners of self-improvement. You can get a free hypnosis download from http://www.RoseannaLeaton.com and peruse her extensive library of hypnosis downloads for hypnosis empowerment.

How To Hypnotize Anyone Through The Power Of Suggestion

by

Jonathan Groves

So, since hypnosis merely creates an altered state of mind, and since hypnosis revolves around the power of suggestion, persuasion can be practiced in many different ways as a tool to change people's behavior. For these reasons, hypnosis is used both in the art of persuasion and in therapy.

Covert hypnosis is the type of hypnosis that is utilized in the art of persuasion. Like any other kind of persuasion, covert hypnosis uses the art of suggestion to give you consistent results. However, because this form of hypnosis is covert, the suggestions that you'll be planting in people's minds will be much more indirect than the suggestions that are installed in people's minds through therapeutic hypnosis.

Covert hypnosis also utilizes all types of suggestion. This means covert hypnosis uses the power of non verbal suggestion even more than it uses the power of verbal suggestion. There can be nothing as under the radar and covert as suggesting something to somebody without having to even say a word to them.

The verbal forms of suggestion that covert hypnosis uses are also difficult to detect. So, instead of saying something to someone directly, you will be saying it to them indirectly to the point where it will not be evident to the person whom you are talking to that you are actually suggesting to them that they do something that you want them to do. This is why covert hypnosis is perfect to integrate into the art of persuasion, because you can modify people's emotions and decision making processes without them being conscious of it. This means it is not likely anybody will try to resist you because they will not have any idea that there are any suggestions for them to resist.

Another powerful hypnosis tactic that can be used is to use covert persuasion to take control of various social structures that exist in any social environment that you may be in. The more power you have over a class system or group, the more it will appear to others that you are a likable person and authority figure. When you appear to other people as an authority figure, your social value increases to the point where people become far more suggestible so that you can get what you would like from them.

Author Resource:- Discover potent covert hypnosis strategies that have been used by the most feared and respected hypnotists to master the power of hypnosis. The power of this hypnosis course has even been used to seduce female prison officers. Download your free persuasion audio now!

Can Hypnosis Really Help?

by

Rachel Ford

Bring up the word "hypnosis" in any conversation and ask people what picture comes to mind. I'm fairly certain they'd immediately summon a rather cliched idea of the hypnotist swinging a pocket watch at a willing victim, telling the subject that they are "getting sleepy".

What transpires after that depends on which film you watched that specific incident in. However as sure as I'm writing this, the hypnotic session would end up with the hypnotist instructing the subject that he will count to three, snap his fingers then the patient would wake up from the trance, often recalling nothing of what happened during the whole incident.

This is what Hollywood hypnotism is, as depicted on the silver screen. Regardless of whether the film turns out to be a massive success or perhaps a great big flop, it has accomplished one thing: It's affected countless people that hypnotherapy can have power over your mind. Then the one hypnotized turns into a slave of the hypnotist and does everything he is instructed only to recall nothing of it after.

In reality, you are rather totally aware of what you are doing whilst in hypnosis. The fact is that you'll never be forced to do anything that you would not ordinarily or willfully do.

During hypnotherapy sessions for healing, whether or not this is you using self hypnosis or it's being done to you by another person, the conscious mind is bypassed to access the subconscious mind. Nevertheless, yet again, you are still utterly aware of your surroundings.

Your subconscious mind processes everything that you hear, see and feel. Every now and then we do not always perceive things with our conscious mind, but it is still being recorded by our subconscious mind.

Hypnosis supports you to correspond directly with your subconscious to transform beliefs or thoughts that will assist you to accomplish a specified objective or goal. In actuality, hypnotherapy assists you override your conscious mind's rigid notions in relation to your life and reset it to process only your desired behavior. It is because your subconscious is considerably more open to solutions than your conscious mind.

If you find that you're frequently feeling distressed and hopeless regarding how things are coming along in life, hypnotherapy can help to change your thinking patterns to ensure that you're able to look positively at life and possess hope for the future.

Hypnosis has also been successful to cause a smoker to start to abhor the smell and taste of cigarettes. In fact, the identical technique applies to those addicted to sweets or candies, along with people who bite their nails.

Another use for hypnosis is to alleviate those struggling with Obsessive Compulsive Disorder or OCD, by helping them acquire a sense of calm and peace when they begin to feel frazzled or out of control.

There are times when fear grips someone so tightly that they're prevented from living their lives to the fullest. A number of examples are: Fear of flying, fear of heights as well as fear of going out in public. Every one of these fears restrict the activities of individuals who have them.

Hypnosis or hypnotherapy can alleviate or remove those irrational anxieties outright by replacing them with feelings that make more sense so that you simply don't have to pass on a normal life. Worry, hopelessness and panic attacks will no longer be a problem since your mind can be reset to react about those fears you had before.

Hypnotherapy affords you a superior possibility at success as it enables you to coach your mind to maintain only thoughts and beliefs which will ensure success.

Author Resource:- Rachel Ford is a Clinical Hypnotherapist who helps people create powerful & permanent changes in their lives. Visit http://www.yourmindzone.com today and download your free hypnosis session.

Common Questions Asked About Hypnotherapy

by

Andrew Bexson

What is hypnotherapy?

Hypnotherapy is a therapy that I use to assist clients find meaningful alternatives to their present ways of thinking, feeling or behaving. Hypnotherapy also tends

to help clients become more accepting both of themselves and others and can be most useful in promoting personal development and unlocking inner potential.

Hypnotherapy is a two way process between clients and myself - a professional partnership.

How does it work?

Once I have gained sufficient information about a client's predicament I will initiate a relaxation from which ideally I will have access to their subconscious mind.

From here I will be in a position to address the issues raised and help their subconscious mind perceive certain events in a different and often more positive light,

while distracting the conscious mind through a series of deep relaxations, thus causing a dissociation between the two states.

Is hypnotherapy safe?

Hypnotherapy is completely safe, non-invasive and a totally natural state. Often It can effectively resolve many challenges, in a few sessions.

Who may benefit from Hypnotherapy?

Everyone can benefit from hypnotherapy, whether a loved one has passed away and you are seeking guidance to move forward, overcome insomnia, gain confidence in order to make a speech, feel relaxed prior to dental treatment, improve a sports performance, overcome anxiety and stress.

Hypnotherapy can improve these and many other ailments.

Do you lose control?

People are sometimes concerned that they will 'lose control' while in a very relaxed state. However, regardless of how deeply they may go into hypnosis and however passive they may appear to be, they actually remain in full control of the situation. Nobody can make you do anything that you do not want to do.

Myths and facts

Myth: A person is asleep during hypnosis.
Fact: A person is totally awake during hypnosis.

Myth: A person in a hypnotic state does not know what is going on around him/her. He/She has totally tuned out the surroundings.
Fact: A person in a hypnotic state can hear everything that they would ordinarily hear. Although he/she most likely has their eyes closed, they are completely aware of their surroundings.

Myth: The hypnotist can make me do things I don't want to do, like take my clothes off or rob people.
Fact: First, an ethical hypnotist would not even ask a person to do these things in the first place. Second: A person has the ability to reject any suggestion(s) that contradict(s) their morals of survival.

Myth: A person loses control of him/herself when hypnotized.
Fact: A person has total control of himself or herself when hypnotized because they choose to hypnotize themselves. The hypnotist simply guides them.

Author Resource:- Please feel free to contact me for questions or further information.

Email: info@lightthewayhypnotherapy.com
http://www.lightthewayhypnotherapy.com

How To Effectively Use Tag Questions in Hypnosis

by

Jimmy Mcintyre

Tag questions, regardless of their simplicity and frequency of use, are very useful tools for influence as they help you to make certain that your listeners are receptive to your ideas. A tag question is simply a negative question hooked on to the end of a sentence. A few examples of tag questions are - Isn't it? Can't you? Haven't you.

To understand the importance of tag questions in developing a more responsive listener just stick one at the end of a sentence and observe how the listener will immediately nod or shake their head (which ever is appropriate) without even know what they're agreeing to most of the time, aren't they?

You may be reading these thinking 'well I use these all the time but I'm not some all mighty master of influence'. This may be true but this article is going to show you how to use them more effectively.

World famous speakers like John Grinder have spoken of this need to get people into a 'yes' set – a receptive frame of mind. An efficient way of doing this is to offer the listener three statements, observations or questions that must be true. Once the client has observed the factual nature of these statements they will start to feel a deeper level of trust towards you and they will have developed into the habit of agreeing with you. Tag questions, in conjunction with other techniques, are wonderful ways of eliciting this state.

To demonstrate this a therapist could say 'you came to see me because you had a problem with X (1st true observation), you had this problem for X months (2nd true observation) and now that we have spoken a little you feel confident we can work together to solve this problem, don't you? (3rd observation).

Useful Tip: To help move a problem into the past the therapist could have said 'you had this problem for X months, didn't you?' This is much more effective than saying 'you've had this problem for X months, haven't you?' or even worse 'you're having this problem, aren't you?'.

You see the importance of using tag questions now, don't you?

To effectively deliver a tag question you must use a lowering command tone as you would an embedded command at the end of the sentence rather than a rising question. Milton H. Erickson, the pioneer of indirect hypnosis and one of the greatest hypnotherapist of all time used tag questions with a command tone regularly as a way of ensuring that his patients were open to his commands. He would often say things like 'and you can…focus more…can't you?' (Notice the use of embedded commands in bold in conjunction with the tag questions). while watching his videos one will often see the subject nodding passively without any resistance.

You can also used tag questions as reinforcement for post hypnotic suggestions. For example, it is more powerful to say 'and you will find more confidence…wont you? than 'and you will find more confidence.'

As you can see tag questions can be an incredibly powerful linguistic tool to help you along the way to persuasion mastery. Strangely enough many people overlook their importance and use more 'complex' language patterns when in reality these can have someone agreeing sooner than another technique, can't they?

Author Resource:- Jimmy McIntyre is the author of http://everydayhypnoticlanguage.blogspot.com/. This is a blog that offers the reader practical everyday examples of hypnotic language patterns. Stop by and offer some language patterns that have been effective for you.

Hypnotic Language: How To Easily Embed Commands

by

Jimmy Mcintyre

The embedded command is a preferred hypnotic language pattern for many and you will see yourself time and time again cheerfully sliding these in and out of your language while getting closer to that increasingly achievable goal.

To begin with - do not try to embed more than 5 words. There's no research to back up the idea of shorter commands being more efficient but using a bit of common sense will demonstrate to you that in everyday life the commands we give to others are often short and concise. And this leads us on to the essence of embedded commands and hypnosis in general; the exploitation of learned associations.

While you're pondering this you may realize that the purpose of an embedded command is to articulate something in such a way that it triggers the same emotional anchor/association that is linked to everyday commands; obedience.

In English this is done by lowering the intonation of your voice towards the end of the sentence. For example, imagine saying 'clean you room' with a question tone (raising your voice at the end of the sentence). Now say it as a command. It's quite a significant difference isn't it? The command tone is what you will subtly use during a conversation to embed commands.

Research has shown time and time again that the brain can establish elaborate patterns that allow you to notice the differences in your surroundings. Why did we evolve this strategy? Well if we consider the good old days when we weren't top of the food chain and a hungry marauder wanders our way we would have been able to survive much more successfully by the ability to notice even the smallest differences in our environment. The predator had a far less chance of getting his grub if the grub spotted him soon enough.

So how to utilize this pattern finding mechanism to our benefit. Firstly you must speak with a fairly constant rhythm. This doesn't mean boring or monotone it just means at particular rate, you can still vary your tone. Fortunately we all speak with our own unique fairly constant rhythms anyway so you don't have to think too much about this. What you do have to consider is how you need to change your rhythms when embedding a command. And this is where the pattern finding machine kicks in. While you're chatting away your conversation partner's unconscious will be very aware of your regular rhythm of speech so when you alter that rhythm it will stand out (also use a very small pause before and after command for emphasis) and once you add a subtle command tone to the sentence the obedience anchor will be fired.

So for a couple of practical examples ...

"(1)Some people find it easy to...(2)go into trance now...(3)and I'm confident that..."

"(1)A person asked me once, 'can you...(2)Embed commands in your language...?'(3) and I said....

Now at step (1) we had normal speaking speed. Step (2) there was a very brief pause, we then inserted the command by slowing/speeding up the speech with a slight command tone. And then in step (3) we started with another very brief pause and began speaking at normal speaking rhythm again.

And hey presto before... you know it...you'll be...embedding commands with greater ease...and I'm not saying you'll...achieve all your goals...but many of them are looking more attainable, don't you...agree?

Author Resource:- I'm the author of http://everydayhypnoticlanguage.blogspot.com where you can find practical every day examples of a multitude of hypnotic language patterns. Why not pay me a visit or even contribute.

Main Hypnotic Suggestions You Should Use In Hypnosis

by

Orik Ibad

Which hypnotic suggestions should you use in hypnosis? Below, I will show six main suggestions and discuss how you can use them in your hypnosis practice.

Here are the six main suggestions.

1. Relaxation suggestion puts you at ease, introduces a state of receptivity and establishes comfortable foundation for further suggestions. It helps you to focus inward while shutting out external conditions.

For example, "Feel your muscle relax and feel your neck and shoulders relax and as they relax you will find your mind relax".

2. Deepening suggestion puts you into a deeper trance. It improves your trance state in a different ways and provides an activity with a single focus.

For example, "Your eyes are closed and they are so shut that you cannot open them. Your eyes are tightly shut, very tightly shut and they are so tightly shut that".

3. Direct suggestion gives you certain actions and instructions which are simple and direct to the point. Direct suggestions are given to respond to the words rather than images.

For example, "You fall asleep gently and quickly, enjoying a restful peaceful sleep, sleeping soundly through the whole night and waking refreshed".

4. Imagery suggestion augments other suggestions. It creates mental pictures and set scenes for specific purposes, such as to relax or to create such environment that all behaviors can be reprogrammed.

For example, "You feel you are as strong as the young man you were when you hit home runs on the sandlot. You can feel the bat in you arms".

5. Indirect suggestions have two major types. In the first type, the desired emotional state is focused on interviewing person's past experience. In the second type, the hypnosis subject is motivated during the induction to relieve the experience and positive emotion accompanied it.

For example, "I wonder how aware you are that many people respect you, and admire you".

Metaphors and analogies are widely used in second type of indirect suggestion to give suggestions outside the conscious awareness of the subject. Indirect suggestions are highly individualized. Each suggestion must fit the subject and his (her) specific problems.

6. Post-hypnotic suggestion is given during hypnosis for an action or response to take place after the hypnotic experience. Post-hypnotic suggestions may be for an action, a feeling or an internal physical change to occur.

For example, "Some time in the next days before the end of the week you will notice a sudden flash of light, or hear an unexpected sound and that will instantly remind you of all you have learned here today and you will be filled with that wonderful feeling of release that tells you will never smoke again".

These are the six main hypnotic suggestions. Use them wisely in your hypnosis sessions and improve the effectiveness of the hypnotic process.

Author Resource:- Orik Ibad invites you to learn more hypnosis secrets on his comprehensive hypnosis site at ===> http://www.hypnosisblacksecrets.com

How Can You Hypnotize Someone Instantly?

by

Orik Ibad

Can you learn to hypnotize others? Or do you need to have special power to do this? Below I will show you 3 simple steps to hypnotize anyone now and instantly. Lets start your hypnosis journey.

Do You Have Hypnotic Power?

Do you need to have special powers to hypnotize someone? Is doing hypnosis difficult? Not absolutely. Hypnotizing others is much easier than you might think. All you need is to learn hypnosis techniques and follow them properly.

I will teach you one of these techniques below and you can apply it on your friends or anyone you want.

Confidence

Confidence is the critical factor for your hypnosis success. If you don't have confidence, then you will probably fail while doing hypnosis. But when you are confident, you will have positive attitude and succeed with your hypnosis practice.

Hypnotize Anyone NOW in 6 Seconds

Now, you have some basics about hypnotizing others. So it is time to start your first hypnosis practice today - right NOW.

You can apply your first hypnosis practice on your friends, parents, lovers and anyone you want. You will be surprised how easy it is.

Firstly, relax the person whom you are going to hypnotize. You must convince your subject that you will not do anything dangerous with her (him). When she (he) is in a relaxed state she will not have fear of anything. And it will be easy for you to apply the technique below on her. This is an important factor.

Could you relax her? OK, then it is time to put her into a hypnotic state. That is what you really want.

Now, follow the steps below carefully:

1- Take one of her arms and ask her to look at your eyes.

2- And you look at her eyes deeply while putting your arm on her neck at least 6 seconds. This will help you to concentrate your subject for the next action.

3- Suddenly cry "SLEEP" and move her head towards you. And you are done. She is now in a hypnotic state. What does this mean? It means that you can now make your commands, offers to her which are called hypnotic suggestions.

This technique is called instant hypnosis induction. Was this process difficult? Not, probably. That is how hypnosis works.

Try this technique on your family members, friends, parents and anyone you want. If you get right education and practice, you will easily hypnotize others. Trust me. Also you should not panic if you fail on your initial attempts. We all passed this step, so don't worry and try it again and again.

Remember: Hypnotizing others is an easy task if you know how to do it. So start learning hypnosis techniques today and follow them with confidence. I guarantee you will you succeed in this way.

Author Resource:- Orik Ibad invites you to learn instant hypnosis secrets to hypnotize someone instantly. You can also learn the basics of how to hypnotize someone on his comprehensive hypnosis site.

Persuasion Techniques--Hypnotic Language Declined

by

Jonathan Groves

Ericksonian Hypnosis failed in the pick up artist community. Women don't use hypnotic language to seduce men. People who are in politics don't use language patterns. Politicians actually say less than is necessary because they like to use the power of scarcity. How long will it take persuasion circles to get it completely through their minds that hypnotic language patterns are a total JOKE?

People are using their appearances, the images they create and portray in public environments, and they are using social strategy to persuade people and get the things they want. Nobody successful is using hypnotic language patterns! Actors are using language patterns, and neither are world leaders using hypnotic language patterns to obtain wealth and power. Most successful and powerful people don't even care about hypnotic language.

When men first began to attempt to go out and seduce women, they tried to use hypnotic language. Needless to say, they became a complete laughing stock. For this reason the male seduction community has changed over the years and moved away from hypnotic language in order to move in the direction of the science of social strategy. Men quickly realized the power of using their behavior to seduce women as opposed to trying to use hypnotic language.

Ericksonian Hypnosis have been scientifically proven to not be able to hypnotize people outside of therapeutic environments. They are not the favored tools for persuasion according to underground hypnosis groups either. Time and time again, ericksonian hypnosis are being shoved back into the clinical settings that they were originally taken from.

Disguised Hypnosis, according to the underground, uses social strategy to take control of and dominate the thoughts of others. The social sciences consist of the professions that comprehend human behavior and who know the theories that govern human behavior. Because of this, persuasion specialists began to integrate the behavior theory of social science into their persuasive tactics to form influential forces that are virtually impossible to reckon with.

Author Resource:- Disguised Hypnosis is the most dominant form of covert persuasion the human race has ever found. The hypnosis secrets enclosed in this program are so shocking they were banned from prison systems across the US. Visit Disguised Hypnosis and down load your complimentary hypnosis CD now!

The Telephone Session

by

Linda Simmon

I have found that each hypnotherapy practice develops a "life" of its own. When I graduated from the Hypnosis Motivation Institute I had no idea that I would have a website, recorded sessions, write a book or do telephone sessions. Over the course of the last several years telephone sessions have taken over my practice. It was the last thing I expected to do and, as it turns out, it is perhaps my favorite part. I have clients all over this country and several other countries as well.

There are, though, certain changes that need to be made when working with a telephone client.

- First of all, I really feel that in order to generate a closer connection, the first session should be a minimum of 90 minutes. You should spend at least 45 minutes just talking to your client and getting to know each other.

- You'll want to length the actual hypnosis portion of your session as well. You will have to spend more time deepening over the phone than you do in face to face sessions.

- And finally, you'll want to spend some time with your client after you have taken them out of hypnosis talking about what they have just experienced. This is something most hypnotherapists do not do during face to face sessions.

As I said, deepening take a bit longer. I have found that an extremely effective technique is to do a series of visualizations each ending with a count down. Each count down takes your client just a bit deeper and after you have gotten to know your client, it makes it easier to have them reach the level of hypnosis that is most effective for the work your are doing. During a first telephone session I recommend doing at least 3-4 images with a countdown.

It is important to listen to what is going on at the other end of the telephone line. If you listen, you'll get a feeling as to how many count downs you'll want to do. Also, keep in mind that you will become more comfortable with each telephone session that you do. After you've done your series of countdowns, it is then time to work with the suggestions that you have developed for their particular issues.

It is also important to make sure that you not only do a count out at the end of your session, but you should do a couple of count outs and reinforce that they are no longer under hypnosis AND that they are no longer suggestible.

Using this technique I have never once not had a client not go under. I believe that clients actually go deeper and are more open to suggestion during a phone session that face to face. I've spend some time thinking about this and I believe it is because they are in their own environment and feel more secure. Even my local clients who insist on an initial face to face session will switch to phone sessions after they have tried one.

If you are still hesitant about doing a phone session, contact me. I would be more than willing to assist you with your first phone session.

Author Resource:- Linda Simmon, C.Ht., is a highly sought after consultant, hypnotherapist, life coach, and speaker. After over 25 years of being a paralegal, she decided it was time to take a new direction with her life. A graduate of The Hypnosis Motivation Institute, the first nationally accredited school for hypnotherapy in the United States and the creator of New Beginnings, Linda is now dedicated to helping people everywhere get a new beginning by helping them break through barriers that are holding and helping them transform their lives. For more information on Linda, her CD's, downloadable sessions, E-Book, workshops and radio show, visit www.newhypnotherapy.com

Section II

Neuro-Linguistic Programming

Libenter homines id quod volunt credunt
"Men gladly believe that which they wish for." Julius Caesar

NLP Anchoring – How to Overcome Cravings and Bad Habits

by

Erika Slater

Anchoring is a key technique used in Neuro-Linguistic Programming and helps people achieve outcomes in life they desire. Here's a quick primer on the topic.

NLP is an alternative therapy that can be engaged to change emotional behavior and achieve self-awareness and effective communication. Examples in the real world include helping with smoking cessation, weight loss and building rapport and relationships.

Anchoring is one of a number of NLP techniques for bringing about significant change in a person's life. Anchoring uses a representation - either internal or external - to trigger a feeling, behavior, or memory. Using the anchor, we can trigger certain behaviors, thought patterns, or emotions, and change aspects of our lives. In fact, we use forms of anchoring all the time.

Here's a common example.

When you drive up to a traffic signal and see a red light, there's a good chance you brake without thinking about it. This is an unconscious process. While you probably had to think hard about it when you first learned to drive, the response is now automatic.

Most of the time, we don't know that anchoring is happening in our lives, since its outside consciousness. However, when we do it on purpose, we can train ourselves to engage in behavior we otherwise wouldn't, such as quitting smoking, becoming comfortable with something that frightens us, or losing weight.

When we come across a trigger, our internal representation systems activate, and there's a response. It could be an action, a memory, or a number of other things.

NLP practitioners tend to look at life as a combination of intentionally and unintentionally selected anchors. From advertisements to the smell of your favorite food, you encounter all kinds of anchors in everyday living.

Anchors can be both positive and negative, and negative anchors can cause real problems for some people. For instance, if you developed a negative anchor relating to something your spouse does, it could seriously hurt your relationship. Your spouse would be triggering bad feelings in you without ever knowing why.

The good news is that NLP anchoring is an excellent tool for tackling stubborn conditions.

When anchoring is performed by a practitioner it's done in steps. First, the specific situation to be triggered by the anchor is induced. For example this may be a feeling of a calm and relaxed state or a feeling of confidence. While in this state the anchor is placed such as pressing fingers together or thinking of a color such as red. The connection between the desired state and the action to induce it each time is made.

Then, the state is interrupted, and the anchor is tested to see if the correct experience has been achieved.

Anchoring is an excellent technique for helping people stop cravings and get rid of bad habits.

Intentional anchoring can be done as part of hypnosis, with a professional hypnotist assisting you. You can also do it on your own and to others in an ethical way.

You probably do it all the time without noticing. Every time you smile and compliment your restaurant wait staff, you're creating an anchor that tells them you're pleasant to serve. The next time you go to that restaurant, you'll probably get better service just by repeating the anchor - a smile and a compliment.

Creating these types of anchors in yourself and others can make a huge difference in your life. You can help people associate your presence with a good feeling, help yourself get around a bad feeling associated with a certain place or activity, or attach a good feeling to a chore or something else that might seem unpleasant.

If you have trouble implanting anchors on your own, talk to an NLP professional, who can help you implant the ones you desire.

Anchoring is one of the most powerful techniques NLP has to offer.

When used correctly, it can change the lives of people suffering from serious challenges. Whether it's a poor self image or relationships, or a bad habit, NLP anchoring can help move a person forward and get the outcomes in life they desire.

The Making of an Effective Anchor

by

Geraldine Paynter

An anchor is an NLP tool used to create a positive state. We respond to anchors all the time, certain foods will get you licking your lips, or a smell of a particular perfume will remind you of your first date, or did you ever get drunk on whisky and now every time you catch the smell of Whisky your stomach somersaults . Our memories are stored as associations with our senses.
The concept of anchoring comes from Pavlov. You remember Pavlov's dogs? In NLP we call what Pavlov did anchoring.

What Pavlov did with his dogs, was that he rang a bell, and showed the dogs food. Rang the bell and showed them food. Then he rang the bell, and the dogs salivated just as if they'd just seen food. The bell (the sound) was actually an anchor. What he had done is to set up an anchor for the dogs. The brain is very good with associating feelings with situations. The brain can attach feelings of terror within a second we know that!

Anchoring is also used by skilful film makers to induce suspense in the audience. Think of your own psychological changes that occurred when you heard the soundtrack's, pounding heartbeat rhythm in the moments leading up to each of the appearances of the huge killer shark in the film 'Jaws.' Did your heartbeat increase? Did you have to see the shark, or was the thumping music enough to start your slide to the edge of your seat?

Sports men and women will frequently use anchors to stimulate a desired state (of confidence, control, calm, etc.) that will help their game.

The anchors can be images, sounds or cue words, or touch/pressure applied to part of your body - they can be internal or external.

The Making of an Effective Anchor

- Making sure the state (emotion) is accessed fully and intensely.
- Getting the client to associate into the state.
- Getting the client to see what they were seeing, when recalling the memory that triggered the state, for this they have to be fully associated into the memory.
- Hearing what they were hearing, again they have to be fully associated into the memory.
- Feeling what they were feeling.

Timing of the anchor

- Start the anchor just before you reach the peak of the experience.
- The most vital portion of the process is to detect where and when the state is at its peak.

The anchor needs to be set just prior to the peak of this state. Make sure that you set the anchor here or you will anchor a state of decline. Time it correctly; you will have anchored a state that is still on an incline.

To create an effective anchor the client has to be fully associated into the state required.

Try this exercise on yourself to create instant self confidence:

Think of a time when you were totally confident, you felt powerful. As those feelings come back to you they will peak and subside. Say the word confidence with a particular, tone, volume and tempo to establish the anchor and start clenching your fist. Repeat this and then test it by saying in the same tone and tempo the word confidence and clench your fist. If you've done it right you should feel a welling up of those same emotions. Simple isn't it?

Timing is crucial, fire the anchors before the peak and release before the peak declines.

Anchors can be visual, auditory or Kinesthetic.

You can use visual anchors to anchor the resourceful state. You can use external or internal anchors. For example, you could use a item of jewellery to anchor being calm and relaxed. The external anchor always has to be there for you to use. You may find it relaxing and calming to view a certain photograph, but unless you can carry it around with you, it is of limited use. You can however use an internal image of the photograph or picture to anchor your resourceful feeling.

Visual Anchors

Most visual anchors are internal. Some examples of visual anchors are:

- Symbols. For example, you could use a circle as a symbol for being calm and relaxed and anchor this to your state.
- People, such as a trusted friend or family member.
- Various objects and landscapes can be used as anchors for being calm and relaxed. For example, you could imagine:
  o A waterfall
  o A flower

Auditory Anchors

You can use a sound as an anchor. Like the visual anchors, sounds can be internal or external. You can use an internal voice as an anchor. For example, you could anchor the phrase 'calm and relaxed' or you could hum.

Remember how you felt as a child when you heard the sound of the ice-cream van?

Kinesthetic Anchors.

- Imagining a comforting hand on your shoulder
- Imagine being comforted as a child, a loving embrace by a parent
- Squeezing the second finger and the thumb together
- Touching yourself on the back of your hand

Visual, Kinesthetic and Auditory Anchors

You could combine the anchors altogether, maybe imagining a loving embrace from a parent, while smelling their perfume and hearing their comforting words, while squeezing your finger and thumb together. Or was it that relaxing holiday with the sound of the ocean, and the smell of the sea air and the warm breeze on your skin.

Setting a Anchor

Ask the client to recall a specific time when they felt confident. You don't want to pick just any old memory of confidence. Pick a memory of a time that they felt extremely confident?
After recalling a specific memory of a time that they were extremely confident, you need to get them to fully re-experience that event.

Get them to really visualise that time.

Ask them to see what they saw and make the colours brighter, ask them to hear what they heard, and to turn the volume up, ask them to feel any of the feelings/emotions they felt,
To take themselves back to that place of extreme confidence in their mind. To feel it, see it and hear it as if it were occurring at this very moment.

As they're re-experiencing the feelings, examine them and then intensify them.

Now the most vital portion of the process is to detect where and when the state is at its PEAK'. The anchor needs to be set just prior to the peak of this state. Make sure that you set the anchor here or you will anchor a state of decline. If you time it correctly, you will have anchored a state that is still on an incline.

The best anchors to use are kinaesthetic ones. Using visual, auditory and kinaesthetic all together, will make the anchor that much more effective. Try to use all three if possible. I call this anchor coupling'. When placing a kinaesthetic anchor, you don't want to place it in an area that is touched frequently. I normally set the anchor on the clients elbow. (I recommend holding it for five seconds) then release it subsequent to the peaking of the state.

When you complete all these steps, you will then need to break state. I suggest going through the anchoring process with your eyes closed. Breaking state will then be easier by just getting them to open their eyes and thinking of something else. Shake it off so to speak.

Author Resource:- http://www.hypnoticgroup.co.uk

Geraldine Paynter has a background in client centered work, with people in crisis and with life shortening illnesses. Has certification in Hypnotherapy, Hypnosis, and NLP. As a full time practitioner has a wide range of experience in treating a range of issues. In recent years Geraldine has developed specialist approaches in a number of areas, these include self confidence, and a unique approach to anxiety related issues.

6 Actions to End Food Cravings Using NLP

by

Evian Gillette

A client wrote, "Help me! I thought I was at last getting a handle on my weight issue nevertheless the sugar is slaughtering me. I had a unpleasant period. I will not even let know you what I ate today since it is simply so unbelievable. All I can say is that 90% of my foodstuff today consisted of sugar! I truly, really need a little assistance getting beyond these food cravings. I am no doubt a sugar addict. If I may possibly progress past this there is no doubt that I can achieve my purpose."

If you witness a bit of yourself inside this letter, you are not alone. Many describe themselves as sugar addicts. They consider if it were being merely for that solitary craze, so therefore they could attain their weight loss ambitions. If you suppose only one thing stands in your road of losing weight, deliberate this: What if that single obsession (an addiction toward sugar for example) ended up being gone? Do you actually consider, "If I may perhaps get past this, there is no question that I can make my purpose," or is it a straightforward justification to stay stuck?

If I informed you I may possibly show you a way to prevent craving sugar, would you require me to show you how?

Think about that for a minute. Close your eyes and really think it through. You've thought if simply you didn't crave sugar, then you can lose weight, however is that if truth be told accurate for you? Ask yourself these questions:

Would you eat differently, as a consequence if so how?

Would you act in a different way, furthermore if so how?

What else would change, and what would stay the same?

What would you lose?

What would you gain?

Until you identify what you desire, know you can accomplish it, furthermore know what in addition can change (i.e. how your life could be different), you can't ascertain any obstacles that at the outset have got to be considered. For instance, you may intend to discontinue eating anything after seven PM yet your spouse does not come home from work until 8 plus he desires you to join him for dinner. That's an obstruction.

If you have acquired a habit of watching your favorite Television show with a bowl of ice cream, subsequently breaking that routine is a further complication.

If you don't work out ways to get over your obstacles possibly throughout debate as well as finding the middle ground with your husband, or habit breaking exercises meant for your ice cream fondness, there's certain to be a dilemma. Solely saying you are not going to do something any more rarely works. Instead find out what might stand in the way of achieving your possible goals, achieve a means around them, and you are a great deal more probable toward truly achieveing those targets once and for all.

The statement, "if this one craze were handled, then everything else would fall into place" is an "If Then" declaration moreover gets people into difficulty. They want a fairy godmother to make it all better. A compelling perception that one single thing such as, "eating sugar is my setback," sets you up to crash, particularly if you genuinely like eating sugary foods.

Getting a grip on your cravings is not a all-or-nothing proposition. You must set aside space for occasional deviations. It really is not the occasional side stumble that creates weight trouble, it really is the highway we tend to frequently travel.

In NLP (Neuro Linguistic Programming) a advantageous starting point is the exercise identified as Establishing a Well Formed Outcome. "Well formed" means it meets all criteria of a well thought-out end end result.

NLP: How to Create a Well Formed Outcome and Obtain What You Want
Here are the procedures toward making a well formed outcome:

1) State what you want (not what you do not want). "I want to weigh 135 pounds."

2) Determine whether you are able to attain it (do you think it is possible?).

3) What resources do you retain also what do you require (time, funds, gear, clothing, equipment, coaching, doesn't matter what).

4) Check whether anyone else is involved and any prospective obstacles that can come up regarding others. Think of everyone involved in your day-to-day life.

5) See in your mind's eye yourself "as if" you have obtained what you say you want and observe if that image fits. Do you like what you observe?

6) Put together a plan of action meant for the achievement of your outcome.

Though it can look akin to a lot of effort merely to conclude what you genuinely would like, going through these actions at the beginning assists you find potential obstacles that earlier stopped you from moving ahead. For example, if you make a decision you intend to join a sports club and start exercising every day but you have forgotten you don't even have a automobile and just lost your occupation, that keep fit plan might not work out just at this time. If you did join a sports center, you'd finish up not going also then you'd think you'd failed, in spite of that it was the plan that failed, not you. You didn't think it through.

A better plan in this instance can be doing work outs at home, otherwise within walking distance (or simply walking for exercise). Later on, when you do obtain transport, you can alter the plan and perhaps join a leisure center afterward. There are forever alternatives.

It really is better to look at what you would like from each angle, subsequently put together a plan you know can and will work. Subsequently when you recognize what you wish for, you will what's more know you can make it come about as well as start through taking that first footstep on the road to making it a certainty.

"Achieving a Well Formed Outcome" is one piece of the missing secret to weight loss. Emotional Eating, as well as food cravings are also taken care of in a new weight loss programme I will tell you about later.

I can't encourage you enough towards losing weight at this time. But if you are still thinking about it, here are a few hard questions meant for you to chew on:

If you don't do something about your weight today, when will be the right time?
If you don't do something about your weight today, what will you weigh next week?
If you don't do something about your weight today, how will you explain still being fat next month?

What you do today creates your tomorrow, so don't delay go lose some weight.

Author Resource:- You're looking to lose weight right! Well if you really want a good program that works and gives you a 100% guarantee CLICK HERE Remember If you don't do something about your weight today, when will be the right time?
Evian Gillette
Easy Fast Weight Control.Com

Do You Listen or Do You Hear?

by

Alistair Horscroft

Lets start this article with a a simple question: "When approached by a colleague, family member or staff member with a problem are you a talker, interrogator or a listener?

With a bit of self awareness it's not hard to see which one we are: Talkers do just that, they just talk.... and talk........and talk. Talkers put up with others speaking just long enough for them to be able to unload what it is they want to say, normally their opinion on to the other person.
Talkers wait for an pause in the conversation so they can say something. Talkers often fake listening just so that they can say something. Talkers speak at people, they do not connect. Obviously talkers are a joy to be around (joke) Talkers most likely have very noisy internal dialogue/self talk. They often either have a misplaced sense of their own importance/sense of rightness or a deep lack of self worth that is overcompensated for by all the talk. They are most often uncomfortable with silence.

Interrogators don't stop asking questions, it's like being with the Spanish inquisition. They want to know everything, every detail, they want to make sure that all the t's are crossed and the i's are dotted as they find out more. Interrogators don't really want to listen, instead they want to gather information for there own self interest. Interrogators often live in a world of hyper comparison, they want to make sure that no one has anything over them. Interrogators often have significant insecurities and believe that by finding out all about you they can assess you correctly, label you and put you in a convenient box (that suits their map of the world). Many people learn that asking questions is a great communication skill, which is true - however there is a very big difference between asking questions out of genuine interest and asking them to satisfy once own psychological complexities and personal insecurities!

Listeners genuinely listen, they want, out of no ulterior motive, to fully understand the other persons needs. Listeners have a well developed sense of self, they respect others opinions, experiences and ideas without judgement. Listeners are able to create a safe environment where others are able to open up and truly be themselves. Listeners have no desire for fake relationships or communication and therefore want others to be themselves as any other form of communication becomes boring and meaningless to them. The Listener is able to create deep trust with others quickly as well as motivate others to talk and share information. Listeners are comfortable with silence and have no need to talk for the sake of it. Listeners truly hear. To create the space where someone actually feels heard is one of the great gifts that you can give to another - it is a rare thing, but a skill worth mastering. To learn to hear is to have mastered one of the most important skills we can for in doing so we provide ourself with proof that we have worked through many of our own personal insecurities and issues. We become more selfless.

Listen to people the way you want to be listened to, and you too will start to feel heard.

8 Barriers To Masterful Listening

1. Doing something else while the person is talking.
2. Waiting (barely) for a pause before jumping in.
3. The need to say something. The inability to remain quiet.
4. Fake listening, something you have to do so that you can talk.
5. Selective listening.
6. Listening only to words rather that the complete person (unconscious signals such as body language and tonality).
7. Easily distracted, can you remain focuses through distractions?
8. Can you be free from judgement - can you dissolve your own world view and personal opinions to remain present?

Article provided by Alistair Horscroft, Director The Mind Institute.
Author Resource:- http://www.themindinstitute.com.au

Section III

The Practice of Hypnotherapy
(In Office and Remote)

Numquam aliud natura, aliud sapientia dicit
"Never does nature say one thing and wisdom say another"

Online and Telephone Hypnotherapy - Successfully Helping Clients Remotely

by

Michael S. Spillan

Hypnotherapy is a complex process which is best undertaken in person, where the practitioner has the benefit of observing the demeanor and expressions of his/her clients[12]. This is, however, not always possible.

Physical restrictions and geographical limitations are just two of the reasons clients may seek out remote assistance. Clients who are unavailable for office visits are just as entitled to the best care we can provide as those who are able to come into offices or clinical workplaces. Sometimes a client will simply need the reinforcement of a suggestion you placed earlier (weeks, months, even years earlier) to prevent a crisis, other times a full electronic intervention may be called for.

I am reminded of a young friend who I had been working through a phobia with. She was unexpectedly called away to help with a familial obligation (due to her grandmother's sudden hospitalization she was asked to stay with her developmentally disabled 50 year old aunt, some 1,100 miles away). Making significant progress, she was reluctant to interrupt her sessions for what would have been months. We continued her sessions by phone for three months, and for one by Yahoo Messenger's Video Conferencing option. We met with great success, finished, and now, nearly a decade later, she is still phobia free.

Some highly effective hypnotherapists have conducted telephone sessions regularly. Thomas Dawes[13], Roberta Temes, Ph.D[14] and Milton Erickson, MD[15] have treated patients thusly, and touted its effectiveness.

There are two different situations we, as hypnotists and/or therapists, can consider. The first is the easiest, established clients who seek the continuation of sessions electronically for whatever reason. The second is the establishment of a series of sessions with new clients. Before we get to these, let me offer some...

General Advice

Remember that during your remote sessions you *cannot* gauge your client's reactions as well as you can in office, so it is essential that the subject knows to interrupt you with necessary information. Explain: "If the way you feel changes, tell me, even if you need to interrupt"; "If you

---

[12] I use the term "client" to refer to both clients and patients.

[13] Early Pioneer in Remote Hypnotherapy.

[14] Author of *The Complete Idiots Guide to Hypnosis* as well as the first textbook on the subject of Medical Hypnosis.

[15] Widely recognized as the Father of Modern Hypnotherapy.

feel yourself beginning to come out of your trance, I want you to tell me immediately, even if you have to interrupt me[16].

As you are not in control of their environment, you also need to tell them that they need to inform you if they become physically uncomfortable for any reason, and, as importantly, that they need to tell you if there are any interruptions (particularly if anyone enters the room).

If you are using Yahoo Video Chat, or some similar option, I advise you to establish a unique ID/Account for just chatting with your patients, and to remain invisible to all clients, except the one you are talking with. I also suggest that your client should establish an account *only* for chatting with you. For prudence sake, make it situational, preventing the trance from taking when driving, and craft it so that your subject will wake immediately if:

1. An emergency arises

2. Someone enters the room - breaking confidentiality

3. The call is disconnected

It is important that the client's situation does not allow for any more interruptions or distractions than your office would.[17] Remember, you cannot control their environment completely when they are not in your office. Most of the things you do to put them at ease in the office, both overt and subtle, will not help. Additionally, you should be cognizant of the fact that there are places in their homes (and elsewhere) which are sources of stress and distractions, ones which they may not even be aware of. If at all possible, you should discuss this with your clients and try to find the place most relaxing and most diversion free for your work.

If you regularly establish deep trances with your client in the office, you will be able to by phone or over the net. Your methods should be the same - keep everyone else out of your office, speak with your client and establish the goals of the trance before undertaking to induce it in them, keep your trances interactive and interesting for both of you, regularly gauge the depth of the trance using deepeners as needed, be sure to bring them completely out of the trance and answer any questions they may have afterward.

There seems to be a tendency to abbreviate electronic sessions. I believe this to be a serious mistake. Make your sessions as complete as you would, rushing remote sessions implies that they are not as important or possibly not as effective as the full in office sessions or conversely, can imply that the full sessions you perform are lengthier than they need to be. For telephone sessions, I suggest that you *do not* make use of speaker phones, on either side of the conversation. On their end, others can listen in, and on your end...well, you would be surprised how well those things pick up background sounds and noise. Headsets, however, are a good idea, though if you use

---

[16] You can follow these with something like "the very act of telling me will return you to your most comfortable and relaxed state, one where you continue to feel safe and enjoy sharing with information with me".

[17] That is to say, none.

Bluetooth or other battery powered ones, be certain of the charge.

Be certain that you keep on top of the depth of their trance.

Professionalism, and consistency, consistency, consistency serve your client the best in office or remote practice.

Treat them as you would in the office and you will do well.

New Clients - Remote Practice All The Way

For new clients I would suggest, if at all possible, that you make use of Yahoo Chat or some similar product, a webcam (at least on their end) and a headset. This will allow you to gauge their reactions depth of trance better than you can by mere phone.

Next, you need to make as thorough an inquiry into their mental/emotional states as you would in the office. Fax, mail or email the same forms and questionnaires you would in office[18] and make sure you have them back and properly reviewed before you begin.

Next explain, in an easy to understand way, how hypnosis works and why your remote client is a good subject. Make sure they are comfortable with you as a person. This is an intimate relationship they are entering into, one probably faster than others of similar intimacy. Remember that they, if they have any understanding of hypnosis at all, know they are making themselves open to you to a degree that they may never have experienced before. You must be reliable, consistent and honest, and you must make sure they understand that you are.

Did I mention that professionalism, consistency, consistency, and consistency serve your client the best in office or remote practice.

Because you cannot as thoroughly evaluate (even on webcam) the depth of trance your client is in, I strongly urge you to use a long induction, one which invokes all of the senses for your first session. Understanding the urge to begin effective therapy immediately, I suggest you ignore it. Instead, I advise that you take time first and establish in your clients mind the depth of session he or she can achieve, and that you put in place 1. A post-hypnotic suggestion that helps them become comfortable with hypnosis and 2. A Trigger phrase that allows you, and only you[19] to quickly induce a deep trance when the two of you are together remotely.

---

[18] It should go without saying that you need to maintain records as detailed (perhaps even more detailed) as you do for office clients.

[19] I am not suggesting that you make it impossible for other qualified hypnotherapists to treat your subject, rather I ask that you make certain that no other person can use the triggers *you* put in place. This will prevent accidental induction of trances *and* will keep your client from inadvertently granting others access they possibly should not have.

Established Clients

"Be Prepared" is the official motto of the Boy Scouts of America, and I suggest that it is one to keep in mind in your practice. The establishment of a post-hypnotic suggestion that allows you[20] to verbally guide your clients into a deep and solid trance over the phone or internet is an exercise in foresight which would impress even the most jaded Eagle Scout.

Let your clients know that remote service may be available for them to take advantage of, and under what circumstances.

Personally, I would not suggest that you offer it to every client. Anyone who is inclined to deep emotional outbreaks during sessions, any new clients uncomfortable with the idea of hypnosis, anyone likely to use, or be under the influence of, any number of mind-effecting medications, and any client who may have a propensity to resist deeper trances should all be carefully screened before considering remote sessions.

Finally, I suggest that in considering whether to make remote sessions a regular part of your practice with established clients, you take care to determine what extra benefit your clients have gained from being in your actual presence. People often build a rapport and take subconscious note of your expressions and mannerisms. With an experienced practitioner these can help put the client at ease, increasing comfort levels and making them more available for therapy.

Odds are that you have created a peaceful and safe environment in your office and the cues they take from it and from your presence cannot easily be replaced by a phone call or video chat. It's best to keep this in mind.

Something you can do, as a part of being a good scout, and being prepared, as a part of the above mentioned induction trigger, remind your client that anytime they are subject to that rapid verbal induction they will "again feel the benefit of the safety and comfort [they] feel with [you] in this office". You have worked hard to create a safe place for them, take advantage of it.

The final thing to be aware of, and to guard against, is that it can be very easy for the remote practitioner to become distracted by things other than the client. Paperwork, TV, a computer, co-workers, texting, anything that you would not let be distractions during an in office session cannot be allowed to become distractions during remote sessions. Your clients, in office or remote, deserve the best you have to give them. Stay focused and make remote practice the best it can be, for your clients and for you!

---

[20] And *only you*, see my note above.

5 Simple Ways to Use Video in Your Hypnosis Business

by

Andrew Wilkie

In this article I'm going to let you know 5 top reasons how you can use video into your hypnosis business and why you should use video.

Hand held video cameras i.e. Flip are easy to buy, use and the finished video looks great. Why wouldn't you want to use video to help market and promote your hypnosis business?

Website Impact
1. The best reason is, so that you can add video to your website. You can record a thanks for visiting message to your customers. After all, you are a real human begin. This also lets customers see who you really are, what you look and sound like. You don't' get to hide behind a website or telephone number. The real you comes across in a video far better than a pre-written email. Most hypnotists are not doing this simple step. Doing so, already puts you ahead of the crowd.

A Business Tour
2. You can record a tour of your business. You can then show potential clients what they can expect from coming to you and being with you. You can hold a customer's hand and set their expectations.

The Pre-Talk
3. Record your pre-talk and give or hand it out to all your clients before they come to you.

Your Safety, Security and As A learning Aid
4. With a customer's OK, you can record your sessions together. Not only does this protect your own safety and that of the customer. You now have an excellent record or your own work that you can learn from and review, show others and use as a training aid.

Create Your Own Products
5. With your own video recordings, you can quickly and easily create your own products to help your customers and other hypnotherapists. Maybe a client can't make it to your office, but they really want to learn how to relax and sleep better. Or perhaps you want to record your stage hypnosis shows? You can create one video and sell it multiple times on your web site, even when you are asleep!

Author Resource:-
To find out how you can get more clients just like the experts Click Here
Claim Your FREE REPORT on How To Use Twitter and Facebook to Promote Your Hypnosis Business from www.hypnosismarketingsuccess.com

Why Every Hypnotist Must Have a Web Site

by

Andrew Wilkie

Are you a hypnotist? Do you know why you must be on-line and have a web site or blog?

Look, I understand. When I finished my training. I knew, I wanted to be on-line and have a website. I just didn't know why or how. Without knowing the why you need to have a website. Your website isn't going to get built and you'll be wasting your cash.

In this article I'm going to give you 5 secrets why you must get yourself on-line and fast.

1. The big old yellow book is dead. I'm sorry, to say it, but placing an ad in the big book, is perhaps the worst thing you can do these days, if you want a return for you advertising money. Yes, have a single line ad, i.e. name, address, telephone number. That's it. The fact is more people begin their research, looking for a hypnotist on-line than anywhere else. It is quicker and easier for a potential client to have a quick search on-line in the office than it is at home.

2. Having a web site or blog is a 24 hour, 7 days a week shop window for you and the services that you provide. In addition, if you have created your own products. They market and sell themselves, even when you don't. You work 5 days a week, 8 hours a day. That is 40hrs a week. Your website works 24hrs a day, 7 days a week, every day of the year. It works 16 hours longer than you do EVERY day.

3. With the internet you can specifically target who does or does not see your adverts and website. You can't do this with print media. Yes, there are specific niche magazines, yet even these aren't specific enough to attract your ideal client.

4. Google - If you type the word hypnosis into Google. All most well known hypnotists have large on-line networks. They have more than one website. Each website points back to their 'main' web site. You can also do this. Building website can be a rinse and repeat process. It can al be done very quickly, easily and cheaply

5. Expensive. It is so easy these days to set-up and host (where your site lives) an on-line presence. You can easily get a quick financial return. Your marketing dollars can go much further on-line compared to off-line. If something fails, you can stop it, change it, and tweak it. You can quickly and easily see what does and does not work for your business, within a matter of hours or days and change consequently. This you can't do anywhere else.

Author Resource:-
To find out how you can get more clients just like the experts claim Your FREE REPORT on How To Use Twitter and Facebook to Promote Your Hypnosis Business from www.hypnosismarketingsuccess.com

Article Submissions For Hypnosis Sites

by

Jon Rhodes

The internet is growing at a rapid rate, and this trend is set to continue for some time yet. There is probably nothing that has revolutionised our lives more since perhaps the creation of the television. Most businesses have cottoned on to this huge global potential, and many have poured massive resources into their online ventures. Hypnotherapists too have acknowledged this potential, and have quickly joined the clamor to have an online presence.

Some hypnotherapists sell their products on line, such as hypnosis CD's, downloads, training courses, books, scripts etc. Others are content to use the web as an information resource for their practice, allowing people to look online for further information when they have read their business cards. Not only can owning a web site broaden a hypnotherapists' client base, it can also give them more credibility, as they can display their knowledge, experience, and professionalism.

What many people notice when they set up their exciting new internet venture is that initially very few people actually visit. You can set up your brilliantly designed site, bursting full of great information and what happens? Very little. Visitors may trickle in at best, and no obvious increases in customers are evident. This can be both surprising and demoralising when you consider that there are many millions of people online.

In order to attract visitors you need to market your site. You need to tell people you are there. Even if you have a great site full of wonderful content, no one will know it is there until you tell them. Just like you could be the greatest football player, singer or actor in the world, if no one knows about you, then the interest just won't be there.

One of the best ways to improve your online venture is to write articles, and submit them to popular article sites, particularly those in your niche. There are several benefits to writing articles to market your website.

It is customary for you to leave a bio and a link to your site at the end of your article. The link is very useful for two reasons. People may like what you have written and decide to click on your link to get to know more about you and your business. They will arrive at your site already with a positive perception of you, and may be more receptive to using your services and buying your products. Search engines also heavily regard links pointing to a site as indicative of a quality and trustworthy site. They send automated 'bots' all around the web, that go around adding up the amount of links you have pointing to your site. The search engines will then promote your site up their rankings the more links you have, giving you even more traffic.

Having many good articles floating around the internet can also help establish you as an expert in your field. It helps build up your trust and reputation, which can't be all that bad for business. People will come across your intelligently written articles and hold you in high esteem. People may even start quoting you within their own articles, and telling each other about you.

Many article submission sites allow people to use the articles you submit for their sites or blogs. Therefore if you write a good quality article, there is a greater chance that other people will take your article and re-publish it on their sites and blogs, with your link and bio still attached. This helps you automatically build even more links to your site over time, and further enhance your reputation.

So why not give it a go? There are many great benefits to article marketing. It builds you direct traffic, helps your site rise through the search engine ranking, and is great for your reputation, and ultimately good for business. Isn't that why you created a website or blog in the first place?

Perhaps I've left one of the greatest benefits until last. It is usually free. It normally doesn't cost you anything, except the time it takes to write the article. This is free advertising that actually has many advantages over paid advertising. Customers will probably warm far more to a well written article offering them help, than a paid for banner or Adsense advert. They can almost feel like they know you when they read your contributions, and will be grateful for any help or inspiration you may have given them. Once you have written an article, you can potentially benefit from it for many years as new people discover it and read it, and new people continue to place it on their sites and blogs. So what are you waiting for?! You have nothing to lose and everything to gain. Give it a go and see what happens!

Author Resource:- Jon Rhodes is a clinical hypnotherapist from the UK. He runs the very popular HypnoBusters hypnosis downloads site. If you would like to promote yourself online, then please click here to add your health links to our growing health directory.

Section IV

Treatment - The Invocation of Change

Transire suum pectus mundoque potiri
"To overcome one's human limitations and become master of the universe."

A Gut Feeling - IBS & Hypnotherapy

by

Sue Preston

Painful and bloating stomach, made worse by stress or eating some kinds of food? You may be suffering from Irritable Bowel Syndrome (IBS).

Most individuals are surprised to learn they are not alone with symptoms of IBS. In fact, irritable bowel syndrome (IBS) affects approximately 10–20% of the general population. IBS is the most common disease diagnosed by gastroenterologists and one of the most common disorders seen by GPs.

Sometimes irritable bowel syndrome is referred to as spastic colon, mucous colitis, spastic colitis, nervous stomach, or irritable colon. IBS is characterised by a group of symptoms in which abdominal pain or discomfort is associated with a change in bowel pattern, such as loose or more frequent bowel movements or diarrhoea, and/or hard or less frequent bowel movements or constipation.

IBS is a debilitating condition and it can have a devastating effect on a sufferer's quality of life. Symptoms of IBS result from what appears to be a disturbance in the interaction between the gut or intestines, the brain and the automatic nervous system that alters regulation of bowel movement.

Clinical hypnotherapy can help people with IBS by significantly reducing stress related attacks. IBS sufferers can also be taught techniques to deal with any symptoms and reduce their onset.

Hypnotherapy is fast becoming the first choice of complementary treatment for IBS because of its excellent results. One clinical trail found that six to eight weekly hypnotherapy sessions greatly reduces or completely eliminates the problem.

Clinical Hypnotherapist, Sue Preston, based in Neath, backs up these findings. Sue has been treating clients with IBS using hypnotherapy and has had excellent results.

Sue commented "Clients enjoy the relaxing hypnotherapy sessions, which are then reinforced by CD recordings to listen to in between sessions. I see clients over a 3 month period, and there is a dramatic difference in their quality of life by the end of their treatment."

Anyone who thinks that they may be suffering from this disorder is encouraged to visit their GP for a proper diagnosis.

Author Resource:- Sue Preston is a Registered Clinical Hypnotherapist, based in Neath, South Wales.

For further information, please telephone Sue on telephone 01639 638033 or visit www.sueprestonhypnotherapy.co.uk

How to Declare Your Independence from Addictions Using Hypnosis

by

John Koenig

Everyone has at least one oppressive habit from which he or she would like to break free. Smoking. Overeating. Drinking too much. Overspending. Exercising too little.

These private tyrants can be every bit as damaging to our happiness as King George's treatment of the colonies. They reduce our strength, consume our resources and limit our growth.

As we celebrate our nation's independence next July, it might be wise to let the spirit of the holiday inspire us to declare our independence from our habits that enslave us. After all, independence is the same concept whether applied to personal dependencies or to the life of a nation. If you look closely, you will see that national and personal freedom have some interesting parallels.

To begin with, the Declaration of Independence was not a spur of the moment decision. As its text points out "mankind are more disposed to suffer, while evils are sufferable, than to right themselves by abolishing the forms to which they are accustomed." There was a lot of suffering that loosened the yoke of British power in colonial America. With the "Intolerable Acts" and other abuses, the colonial leaders gradually came to believe that the evils of British rule had become insufferable. Only then did they give up trying to compromise and declare independence. As they wrote, "Our repeated Petitions have been answered within repeated inquiries." Their only choice was revolution.

This desperate emotion is known as "hitting bottom" when it starts a personal revolution to free us from victimization by our unhealthy habits. Any important change requires a strong emotional commitment. A person must accept the unacceptability of the habit. They must also be angry enough to do something about it. Occasionally, I see people in my hypnotherapy practice who think they should quit smoking, stop drinking, start exercising or make any of a dozen other habit changes without this gift of desperation. They aren't happy about the problem. But they are not sick and tired enough to do something about it. Like the loyalists during the revolution, they still cling to their habit as a comforter, friend or just part of the way they are. No one makes a significant change in their life because other people think they should. We must be the ones to take a stand for our own health and wellbeing. No one else can do it for us. The colonists had to do it for themselves. So do we.

A distinguishing feature of the US Declaration of Independence is that it not only ended something (British rule), but also introduced a new idea into world consciousness. The vision was, is, and hopefully will always be "that all men are created equal, that they are endowed by their Creator with certain unalienable Rights, that among these are Life, Liberty and the Pursuit of Happiness" and that governments derive their "just power from the consent of the governed" opened up new, and very exciting, possibilities for all humankind. The Patriots weren't only fighting for an end to abusive domination by men in red coats from across the ocean; they were fighting for an ideal. This added dimension made the American Revolution a cause worth dying and living for. Though the Declaration of Independence mentioned numerous grievances, its significant legacy is the ideals that still inspire Americans today.

It is very important when starting a personal revolution that you develop this added dimension. You don't want to quit something. You want to see yourself as becoming something new and better. We experience quitting something we think we like (e.g. smoking, overeating, drinking alcohol, and taking drugs) as deprivation. And people, especially in today's instant gratification culture, hate the idea.

No matter how much pain a habit causes us we will stick with the addiction as long as it doesn't hurt too badly. This is why therapists and other coaches help people develop substitute new behaviors and rewards that are themselves gratifying. In hypnotherapy, we begin with a new positive, healthy vision of the client as a non-smoker, sober and clean man or woman, moderate eater, health-oriented moderate eater, enthusiastic exerciser or whatever the desired change is. Personal change can be a joyful experience provided we allow it to be so.

The colonial leaders had reached a point in the mid 1770s where they felt that half measures would avail them nothing. They saw themselves at a turning point and chose to make a clean break with their overseas' masters. They left no room for ambiguity when they declared "That these colonies are, and of Right ought to be Free and Independent States: that they are Absolved from all Allegiance to the British Crown and that all political connection between them and the State of Great Britain is and ought to be totally dissolved." When they signed these words they literally committed their lives to the cause of freedom. If the revolution failed they knew they had just signed their death warrant.

To free oneself of an addiction begins with a similar bold declaration that the person has gone to war with the habit and intends to separate from it absolutely. Those who allow themselves to hold out a way back have a much harder road than those who simply say I am through with this. I no longer want this addiction (habit) in my life. The alcoholic who accepts that one drink is too much and a thousand is not enough is on the road to recovery. Smokers, or other drug addicts, who understand that one cigarette will likely get them hooked again, save themselves the trouble of reaching new, lower bottoms. The overeater who allows himself or herself little treats whenever life seems too bleak or demanding has already lost the battle. It is just a matter of time before they are back where they started.

It is interesting that we celebrate July 4th, 1776 as our national Independence Day rather than when the date in 1783 when the Treaty of Paris was signed and Britain formally conceded America's independence. After all, on July 4, 1776 America was definitely not free of British domination. Americans used British currency. British soldiers were garrisoned throughout the colonies. Our practical day-to-day government was under British control. Our official church was The Church of England whose head was King George. And, as much as 1/3 of our population was adamantly opposed to independence. They considered themselves loyal to the Crown and would even fight for their beliefs. But, in a very real sense, The United States Independence did begin that July 4th. Because we declared ourselves free, we were free. True, it required effort and perseverance to make our freedom a practical reality. Yet from this point onward we were a nation.

The power of a declaration is that it stands on its own without evidence. When a person declares himself or herself a non-smoker, their friends and family adopt a "wait and see" attitude. There may still be a world of repercussions from the active addictions. Bills unpaid. Health problems from mild to life threatening. Legal issues unsettled. Personal relations damaged. And, yes, a diminished self-esteem. But by taking steps and persevering, reality eventually gets in step with the change. Coaches, therapists and other support people, myself included, help the habit changer map out a plan for change. We then encourage them to follow the plan never forgetting the clear vision of their personal declaration of independence.

So, when in the course of human events, we reach a point where we are no longer willing to pay the price for our habits or addictions, the first step is to make a Personal Declaration of Independence. Declare yourself free of this addiction once and forever. The second is to begin to live, as though it were so one day at a time. As we would say in 21st century America "fake it till you make it." As Thomas Jefferson said, "Do not expect to be translated from despotism to liberty on a featherbed." The third step is to get help. The United States didn't gain independence without substantial assistance from both Spain and France. It made us no less independent of Britain that we had allies. Nor will it make you any less independent of your habits to work with a professional, join a group, or just enlist the help of a close friend.

The fourth step is to continue to celebrate your independence. Habits have a way of sneaking back when we least expect it. Just as the British decided to try to regain their "colonies" in 1812, addictions lie in wait looking for a moment of weakness. Be grateful for the change and be vigilant for any threats against your independence. Get it right and you can look forward to happy Independence Days in the years to come.

How hypnosis and a hypnotist can help

Hypnosis can be the shot heard round the world in your personal life. It can be the impetus that pushes you out of complacency into action. And it can strength your motivation and belief in your own ability to success. It can also make the old habits seem unpleasant and instill new positive ones in their place.

So, why not start your personal revolution today. Take your best shot. Call a hypnotist or start with a self-hypnosis recording. You have nothing to lose, except your chains.
Author Resource:- For more information on transformational hypnosis,visit my website at http://www.possibilities.nu/hyp.htm

Hypnosis to Heal Male Rage

by

Bryan Knight

Anyone can become enraged once in a while. But if you feel rage boiling within almost constantly, or rage erupts from you frequently, you may have an organic illness.

On the other hand, you might have suffered some terrible injustice as a child.

One major, but largely ignored, category of such abuse is that of boys emotionally, physically, or sexually damaged by women.

This abuse is not only widespread but may be at the root of much subsequent abuse of women by men.

A little boy abused by a woman suffers in similar ways to a little girl abused by a man.

In recent times it has become acceptable for women to speak out about the abuse they suffered as children; most men feel no such permission is given to them about the abuse they suffered as little boys at the hands of women. These men are ashamed, and enraged.

They are enraged because society accepts that men can be angry but there is less acceptance for the male victims' feelings of hurt, fear, inadequacy, guilt, embarrassment, and especially weakness and vulnerability.

A male victim smothers these emotions with anger. In this way, he preserves his masculine image. But the cost is enormous.

A man unaware of the deep sources of his anger will, at the least, have troubled relationships with women; at the worst, he may rape and mutilate.

A male victim of childhood sexual abuse by women displays the following behavior as an adult:

>> Distrust of women.
>> Fear of intimacy.
>> No separate identity.
>> Readily feels guilt.
>> Hard time to accept compliments.
>> Holds back emotions.
>> Protects abuser(s).

\>> Sexual difficulties.
\>> Seeks abuser's approval.
\>> Constantly apologises.
\>> Fearful.
\>> Eager to care for others.
\>> Joyless. (Adapted from Blanchard, 1987*)

The lousy feelings often erupt as rage. Ronald sought professional help to change his vicious behavior toward his wife, Helen.

Ronald would arrive home disgruntled after a disappointing day (every day was disappointing) in the architectural office where he worked, and an hour's drive to the suburb.

Before long, he would be kicking Helen. There was always some pretext for the kicks. (Helen did not have supper ready, or she was on the phone, or she wore a dress he hated...). Ronald never used his fists. Always his legs. He despaired of his uncontrollable rage because he believed that "Helen was the best thing that had ever happened to me."

As Ronald talked more about his life, his hostility to almost everyone became evident. He was jealous of his brothers, sneered at their choices of wives, hated his job where he felt put upon, especially by female colleagues.

When Ronald spoke about his mother, he whined. Long stories of how she favored one or other of his brothers, how he cringed in her presence, how he avoided visits to her house yet was jealous of her contacts with his siblings. Ronald was convinced his mother preferred one of his nephews, adding bitterly, "Though my son was the first grandchild."

Hypnotherapy Heals the Hurt and the Rage

Within the comfort of hypnosis Ronald was able to connect his present-day woes with unpleasant incidents in his childhood.

This was accomplished with what hypnotherapists call an "affect link." You allow yourself to feel a particular emotion, such as grief. As you continue to experience the feeling, the hypnotherapist asks you to recall an earlier time when you felt the same way. Ronald's confused mix of bitterness, rage and sense of abandonment, swiftly drew up a memory of his mother:

"I'm six years old. Mummy keeps telling me I'm her favorite. She tells me to come into her bed. It's warm there. I fall asleep, snuggled beside her. I wake up. She's moving my leg up and down over this hairy place between her legs. She's breathing funny. I'm scared. [Sobs]. She opens her eyes a little and tells me it's okay. My knee is wet. I try to pull away but she holds onto me, tells me to be a good boy, do this for Mummy. She seems out of breath. I'm scared. Then she shakes and cries out. I'm even more scared and I feel bad, like something's really wrong. I ask Mummy if she's all right. She turns to me with a big smile, hugs me and says I'm her little man and everything is fine. [More sobs, reddening of face].

"But everything is not fine. I don't understand. Mummy tells me this will be our special secret. She seems happy. And she likes me best. So I keep quiet. And whenever she asks me I let her use my leg to rub her where she wants. [Later Ronald described other sexual activity his mother initiated]. I begin to like it, too. When I get old enough to have an erection, Mummy plays with my penis. I really like that. But at the same time it feels kind of weird. This stuff went on till I was eleven. I found out at school what sex was supposed to be, and how bad it was what Mummy and me had been doing. I felt sick."

With psychotherapy while he relaxed in hypnosis, Ronald made some progress toward a healthier life, and control of his rage.

Unfortunately, his wife sabotaged the treatment. Ronald, like many sexually abused victims, had (unconsciously) sought out a woman who would continue the abuse he had suffered as a child.

Helen had made no secret of her broad sexual experience prior to meeting Ronald; indeed, she was proud of it. But her knowledge of the carnal world and his relative innocence (sex with only one woman: his mother) repeated the power pattern Ronald had suffered as a boy.

When Helen saw that Ronald was learning to control his rage, to lessen his hostile attitude and to relax, she counterattacked. Helen had married Ronald because (unconsciously) she wanted a man she could dominate and despise. His therapy threatened to upset the delicate dance of danger they had created.

Ronald was swiftly reduced to a sniveling, angry puppet when Helen sneered at his progress and repeatedly reminded him of what a Mummy's boy he had been.

A final blow bounced Ronald out of therapy: Helen telephoned the therapist, discussed Ronald's history, and insisted the therapist not mention her call to Ronald. The following week Helen casually mentioned to Ronald something the therapist had said to her. Ronald felt betrayed [he was] and never returned to therapy.

You may be doing very well with hypnotherapy when a friend or relative sabotages your progress. This is not usually as dramatic or underhanded as Helen's behavior. The disruption comes in the form of doubt. Your friend may question the effectiveness of hypnosis, and cite the many hypnosis myths that still pollute our minds.

Once doubt is planted, hypnosis ends. Doubt and fear keep us from relaxation. And relaxation is the route into hypnotherapy.

Dennis, like Ronald, suffered fits of rage. Unlike Ronald, Dennis took these fits out on himself. He would tremble, and shake, and sweat and fear he was about to pass out. Dennis knew his ambition to become a police officer would never be realized unless he got over these fits. Like Ronald, he had troubled relationships with women.

Unlike Ronald, Dennis had slept with dozens of women. All his longer-term relationships collapsed over an aspect of jealousy, his or hers. Didn't matter. Dennis could not trust a woman.

Dennis deliberately sought out a male psychotherapist who sometimes used hypnosis. But so scared was Dennis of going into hypnosis, that he spent several sessions in traditional psychotherapy before he had plucked up enough courage to try hypnosis.

Mothers Are Not The Only Women Who Abuse Little Boys

As far as Dennis knew, he had not been molested by his mother. Actually, he was not even sure who his biological mother was. He had been born into a large, extended criminal family. He had lived in seven different homes by the time he was five. All but one were homes of his aunts, cousins or siblings. He got used to calling each aunt in turn "mother." The woman listed on his birth certificate showed no more, and no less, maternal interest in Dennis than did any of her sisters who raised him.

From as far back as he could remember, Dennis had been abused: abandoned, ignored, ill-fed, beaten, locked in a closet.

The therapist helped Dennis sort out the multitude of feelings that swirled within him.

Finally, Dennis said he was ready to try hypnosis. He was still frightened, despite the therapist's explanations about the safety of the process. But it was not hypnosis itself that Dennis feared; it was what might be uncovered.

In one way, he was right to be wary. But what was uncovered, awful as it was, freed Dennis from the last symbolic chains that linked him to his abusive family and their criminal ways.

In hypnosis, Dennis traced his attacks of trembling to some disgusting sexual behavior of one of his aunts when he was about four. What she had done to him and with him amounted to torture. It had been so horrible he had repressed the details for years, though "I knew something had happened; I just didn't know what."

Now that he knew what lay at the root of his rage and his attacks, Dennis was able to let go of them. He felt forgiveness for his aunt because he knew of her own dreadful background. It was as if to know what she had done liberated Dennis from any lingering loyalty to his criminal relatives (all of whom were involved in drug deals, prostitution, extortion, etc.).

Now Dennis felt fully comfortable with his decision to apply to the local police training college.

Hypnotherapy had not only uncovered the causes of Dennis's rage, but enable him to find release and peace.

*Blanchard, Geral. (1987). Male Victims of Child Sexual Abuse: A Portent of Things to Come, Journal of Independent Social Work, 1-1, 19-27.

Author Resource:- Bryan M. Knight, MSW, PhD, specializes in freeing adult survivors of childhood sexual abuse from their legacy of horror. **http://www.therapy-insights.com/Overcoming_Childhood_Sexual_Abuse.php**

What to Expect During a Hypnotherapy Session

by

Brenda Matthews

In the first hypnotherapy appointment count on to have a pre hypnotherapy dialog for a lengthy interval of time. It is vital that the hypnotherapist has a full understanding of the condition that you simply endure out of and it really is implications.

He would need to get a full understanding as to how the situation impacts your life and in what way. If for instance you go see him for quitting smoking hypnosis then you can expect that she or he will need to attempt to find out the triggers for your dependancy, when you smoke, how usually, if you began initially and when you smoke all through the day.

The hypnotherapist might attempt to search out out what if something, usually are behind the smoking.

It can at instances be a little irritating for the client when the therapist asks so numerous and prolonged questions but its essential for the consumer to understand that the more info the therapist has, the more probably he'll be capable to treat the situation successfully.

After this interview, the hypnotist may run a couple of suggestibility checks that may outline how suggestible you are. There aren't any right or wrong answers to those indicators so do not be ashamed if they don't seemingly 'work'. It's always not their purpose. The outcomes will give the hypnotherapist several ideas as to how finest to hypnotize you.

Following that, he'll begin the hypnosis.

After the hypnosis it might be best to anticipate being all completed up for that session and to make an appointment for next week if the hypnotherapist think it vital - typically it can be.

The vital thing to notice with most hypnotherapists could be that almost all imagine that if you can't be 'mounted' or moved in the suitable route by hypnosis, that it really is vital that the shopper not be strung along.

It sometimes takes 1 to 5 sessions to repair or cure the commonest circumstances, if outcomes cannot be achieved after 5 classes I would search for one other hypnotherapist or one other modality to assist me move forward in life.

Author Resource:- Find out more about clinical hypnosis at hypnosis melbourne.

Stress and Hypnotherapy

by

Michelle Chapple

There are many definitions of stress and to understand what it is can help us understand how to deal with it. One definition is that it is the physical and mental 'wear and tear' we experience as we attempt to cope with the pressures in our lives. Another definition of stress is that it is a physical and mental response to too much or too little pressure.

Many would assume that those with too little pressure are unlikely to suffer stress but this is not true, in fact if you look at stress in organisations it is not higher management who suffer stress most but it is those who have less control over their environment.

A third definition is that stress can be caused when there is high demand, high restriction and low support which means if you are expected to do too much with too little resources and with insufficient support you may be prone to stress.

The typical physical symptoms may include palpitations, increased pulse rate, sleepiness, chest pains, pins and needles, weakness, dilated pupils, insomnia, fainting, butterflies, tightness in chest and an increased frequency in using the toilet. The psychological reactions to stress can include feeling under pressure, constant fear, increased irritability, proneness to tears, impulse to run and hide and high sensitivity to external stimuli.

Another reaction can be to develop irrational fears such as the fear of death or of social embarrassment. Another quite important reaction can be the inability to enjoy any present pleasures like people who go on holiday and come back more tired and stressed than before they went.

It is estimated that about 40 million working days are lost in the UK as a result of stress- related illnesses and the cost of this absenteeism is in the region of £1.5 billion per year. Such illness could include migraines, digestion problems, insomnia, rashes, exhaustion and even alcoholism.

The medical profession estimate that almost 80% of modern diseases have their origins in stress. Many common illnesses which can be triggered or worsened by such as asthma, diabetes, ulcers, IBS, skin complaints, headaches, PMS and depression.

Stress can also cause damage to our immune systems by affecting the thymus gland, which manufactures white blood cells, called T cells, and also produces various immune-related hormones. Stress plays a big part in coronary heart disease, our biggest killer, which is responsible for over 250,000 deaths annually in the UK and is the single most common cause of death in the developed countries.

There are many different causes of stress but broadly speaking they can be split into two basis categories – external and internal stressors. The external stressors would include major life events such as the death of a relative, losing your job, having a baby, dealing with a traumatic incident or even being promoted.

Physical things around you such as noise, heat, bright lights can affect you as well as how you interact with others e.g.: associates being bossy, rude or aggressive. Rules, regulation, 'red tape' and deadlines as well as commuting, losing things or even a mechanical breakdown all count as external stressors.

Internal stressors may include not enough sleep, too much work, caffeine, being too self- critical, over-analysing, or being a perfectionist. Other examples would include having unrealistic expectations, all-or-nothing-thinking, taking things personally, exaggerating, rigid thinking or being a workaholic.

You may not think suffering from stress does not really matter but it can be more serious than you think. Prolonged stress can lead to burnout, post traumatic stress disorder or in its worst form it can produce biochemical changes which can burn out the nerve endings at the top of the neck which can effect the mobility in your body.

One factor that many do not consider is that in a strange way stress can be infectious. If your parents were stressed when you grew up or if friends or work colleagues are stressed you can inherit their stress. If you think of stress as if it were a virus that you have to protect yourself against then it becomes far easier to manage. However stress is not all bad, in fact we all need a certain amount of stress to help drive us through our lives and without it could be just as bad as having too much.

Stress can be treated and with professional help usually quite quickly. It involved sitting down with an expert and talking through any issues you may have and making a plan. You may also be taught techniques that will help you focus more and relax in a different way. There are also techniques that will help you feel better about yourself and your life.

Using hypnotherapy combined with stress counselling is often the quickest approach and is safe as it does not require drugs which may have side effects and research has shown that people with stress or mild or medium depression should be given talking therapies before going down the drug route.

Powerful new treatment for stress

It had been long known that there are three main way of trying to address stress – the physical approach e.g.: the psychological approach using a talking therapy such as stress counselling and hypnotherapy, physical approach using therapeutic massage or drug therapy. Most agree that the drug approach is the most risky as there are risks of side-effects and drugs without a talking therapy will not address the issues so likely to be a short term fix.

So in the past people suffering from stress might opt for stress counselling and hypnotherapy or therapeutic massage therapy. Now a dynamic new therapy has been launched which offers a combination of self-hypnosis and a therapeutic massage available in clinics or spas.

Hypnotherapy

Hypnotherapy has become very popular over the past ten years since the publication of numerous medical studies some only possible thank to the recent development of high powered CT scanners. Experts in the US, UK and around the world have shown that hypnosis can help to activate different parts of the brain and the outcomes can be very positive.

A dramatic shift came about thanks to the research of Professor Peter Whorwell in the UK, Professor David Spiegal at Stanford University in the US and other top experts around the world who have looked a numerous uses for hypnotherapy as a safe alternative to other medical treatments.

Its benefits in treating stress have been know for decades but in recent years research has also shown it is very useful in treating common conditions such a IBS (Irritable Bowel Syndrome) which as many as 1 in 5 people are believed to suffer from. Even NICE (the independent body of experts who evaluate treatments in the UK) have been forced to amend their advice to doctors to include hypnotherapy which suggests soon it will cease to be considered as a complimentary treatment but mainstream.

In addition to IBS and similar stomach disorders hypnotherapy is known to be helpful in treating a number of medical conditions and it is also used for safely reducing pain for people with long term pain (eg: arthritis) and making childbirth less painful and reducing the need for pain killers that may have harmful side effects.

It has been used for psychological issues for many years such as treating phobias, changing learnt behaviours, recovering lost memories and treating insomnia. Also it has proved very effective in safely helping deal with addictions such a smoking, alcohol and drugs.

For several years now medical schools around the UK have offered training modules in Hypnotherapy which have been well received by young doctors and there is now an association for medical students and doctors who are involved in medical research using clinical hypnosis (www.msha.org.uk) which shows how times have changed.

Massage Therapy

There are a wide range of massage therapies available which for many years have been proven to help people with a wide range if muscular or bone conditions cause by disease or injury. It is also know that massage is enormously helpful in relieving the physical symptoms of tension and stress. There are a wide range of therapeutic massages available which range from more medical interventions such as physiotherapy which you can get through your GP or hospital to some of the more relaxing treatments such as Aromatherapy (using special healing oils) and general massage.

The Mind and Body Therapy massage has been devised by an experienced Chartered Physiotherapist to compliment and enhance the psychological benefits of the Mind and Body Therapy self-hypnosis protocol. When given by a MaBT trained and licensed massage therapist the two powerful treatments will be synchronised to provide an amazing experience.

The MaBT massage treatment typically takes about 45 minutes and the massage is very gentle. There are two stress protocols one where you lie on your back and the other where you lie on your front most will book both treatments for maximum effect.

The Mind and Body Therapy protocol for Stress was been piloted at the Orchard Clinic near Pangbourne in Berkshire with outstanding results. It has been developed by a top therapist specializing in stress counselling and medical hypnotherapy and a chartered physiotherapist.

Over a six month pilot period this year all those receiving this new combined therapy have reported a massive reduction in stress levels even after just one treatment. Many clients saying this was the most relaxing therapy they have ever had and a truly amazing experience.

The therapy is now being rolled out around the UK and a home version of the stress protocol is available on CD at cost of £15. Over the next 12 months new MaBT treatments for IBS, pain reduction, insomnia and other conditions will also be available through all MaBT appointed clinics and spas. Go to www.mindandbodytherapy.co.uk for full details.

Christopher Morgan-Locke is the founder of Mind and Body Therapy and is the Clinical Director of The Peel Clinic which is based in London (Clapham Common – Battersea and also operates in Surrey and Hampshire. Got to www.thepeelcinic.org.uk for full details.

Author Resource:- http://www.thepeelclinic.org.uk

Hypnosis And The Fear Of Crowds

by

Jon Rhodes

The fear of crowds is an anxiety disorder which can severely limit the lifestyle of the sufferer. Those who suffer from a fear of crowds often have several symptoms when in or approaching a crowd. These include heightened alertness, increased anxiety, nausea, headaches, excessive sweating, shortness of breath, shaking, chest pains and more.

This leads to those who have a fear of crowds avoiding situations where they may have to confront there fears. Crowded places such as public transport, shopping malls and busy streets are avoided at all cost. If this fear is left untreated, sufferers can find smaller and smaller groups of people affecting them to the point that they no longer leave the house. This is why it is so important to treat a fear of crowds quickly and effectively.

A cycle of fear is created, whereby a sufferer will feel fear when in a crowd of people, and leave in a frightened state. This tells the subconscious mind that you were just in a dangerous situation. Next time you are in a crowd, the subconscious remembers this, and creates even more fear than the last time, in order to help meet your survival needs. This can cause you to be more fearful, and run away sooner when there are less people around than before. This cycle can continue many times, making the sufferer more and more fearful each time.

Hypnosis is a very effective tool for relaxation. It can help calm both the mind and body. A clinical hypnotherapist will typically relax the patient before gradually introducing suggestions of being around people. He will guide you to imagine being round a small amount of people. The hypnotherapist will then gradually increase the number of people when he is sure you are calm and relaxed before each incremental increase. This teaches the subconscious mind that it does not experience any dangers or alarms when around people, and thus breaks the cycle of fear.

The subconscious thinks that it has experienced a situation where you were in a crowd and there were no dangers or fears. The subconscious mind does not know the difference between what it has actually experienced, and what you imagined in trance. Therefore it can quickly grow in confidence that it is perfectly safe to walk amongst people in a crowd.

This is a really effective method of treatment, and borrows from the psychological technique of systematic desensitisation. This is where a patient is gradually introduced to a fear stimulus one step at a time. In this case you might walk to the bottom of your street and back. Then you might go into a small shop, and so on, until you are in a busy shopping arcade with hundreds of people around you. Hypnosis has the advantage that you don't need to go out and find differing sizes of crowds for you to graduate up to, which is practically almost impossible in the real world.

Hypnosis has a strong scientific foundation, and is tried and trusted by many people around the world. Hypnotherapy is not just confined to stage hypnotists turning people into chickens. It is a safe, powerful, and popular form of therapy which can help transform people's lives in a positive way.

Author Resource:- Jon Rhodes is one of the UK's leading clinical hypnotherapists. Click here for more details on his hypnosis audio session to help treat fear of crowds. Click here for more details on his HypnoBusters hypnosis download site.

Get Beautiful Skin With Hypnosis

by

Jake Rhodes

It is said that the quality of your skin is a reflection on your inner health. So if you find yourself with skin problems such as acne rosacea, flakiness or psoriasis it may be that you have an internal imbalance. There are many skin creams, scrubs and various other products on the market but these tend to be expensive and ineffective. The reason they don't work is that they may cover the skin but they don't treat the internal imbalance. It's like covering a bruise with a band aid, it might hide the bruise but it does nothing to make it better.

How then do you get to the root of bad skin? The answer may surprise you, but hypnosis is scientifically proven to vastly improve skin quality. Just how though does hypnosis work to give you better skin?

Hypnosis excels at dealing with internal imbalances because it works on a subconscious level. When you try hypnosis for yourself you might be surprised by the experience. You are not asleep or under the control of the hypnotherapist. Instead you enter a deep state of relaxation where the hypnotherapist guides you through a script designed to improve any aspect of your being that you want. In this case your skin. You cannot be stuck in hypnosis, and almost anybody can be hypnotized.

Most skin conditions are a result of diet and stress. Both these issues can be treated very successfully by hypnosis. A skilled hypnotherapist can plant suggestions into your subconscious mind to avoid unhealthy foods which negatively affect your skin's health. By replacing high-sugar/salt foods with fruit and vegetables you will see a noticeable improvement in the quality of your skin.

However hypnosis also goes one step further. No matter what you use hypnosis for, you will be amazed at just how relaxed and stress free you will feel afterwards. If you've ever meditated then you know just how rested you feel afterwards, and hypnosis leaves you with a very similar feeling. So when you try a skin hypnosis session you are both improving your diet for the future and relieving any stress you hold.

By now you might be thinking "This all sounds great, but I can't afford a hypnotherapist!". The great thing is that nowadays getting a high quality hypnotherapist to treat you is within the financial reach of anyone. There are a number of excellent hypnosis sites on the internet run by popular clinical hypnotherapists who offer sessions that cost around $10 to $20.

The reason hypnosis mp3s are so fairly priced is that a hypnotherapist can take the time to record one session, and that session can then be sold to potentially thousands of customers. Due to this you can find hypnosis mp3s that will give you healthy, clear skin without damaging your bank account.

Just imagine being able to look in the mirror a few weeks from now and seeing a face with beautifully clear skin smiling back at you. You can make that image a reality through the stunning power of hypnosis.

Author Resource:- HypnoBusters are one of the leading online hypnosis resources. They provide articles, videos and many hypnosis mp3s that have been professionally recorded by clinical hypnotherapist Jon Rhodes.

You can improve the quality of your skin in the comfort of your own home with our skin hypnosis mp3.

Get Beautiful Skin With Hypnosis

by

Jon Rhodes

Hypnotherapy is well known to help with many issues such as weight loss, phobias, confidence issues, and addictions such as smoking. Creative and inventive hypnotherapists have greatly expanded this traditional base of therapies, and now the latest trend seems to be hypnotic botox sessions.

An actual Botox procedure works by a series of small diluted botulinum toxins' being injected into various muscles in the face. These injections have the effect of relaxing the facial muscles, causing wrinkles to relax and soften. The effects usually last between 4 and 6 months, when another injection may be required. However it is often the case that after each injection the wrinkles return as less severe, as the muscles are trained to relax, giving some permanent benefit.

Botox blocks the transmission of acetylcholine from the nerves to the facial muscle. Acetylcholine is a neurotransmitter which sends a message to the muscle telling it to contract or tense up. When the flow of acetylcholine is reduced, the muscle can no longer retract and it relaxes. As a result, any wrinkled areas smooth out and soften.

Hypnosis is very effective at replicating this effect, but without the need for an expensive procedure that caries a small, but albeit realistic risk. Hypnosis is very effective for relaxing both the mind and body. A good clinical hypnotherapist can direct a subjects' attention to relax specific muscles, anywhere in the body. The hypnotherapist only needs to direct a subject to relax the muscles in the face, and the results are very similar to a botox operation – a relaxation of the facial muscles, which leads to a smoothening of the lines and wrinkles in the face.

A hypnotherapist can teach a patient self hypnosis so that they can use it to top up the initial therapy. A patient can then hypnotise themselves every few weeks in order to maintain the muscle relaxing, facial smoothing effects. A person using audio sessions can simple re listen to them every now and then for no extra charge, helping to keep those facial muscles nicely relaxed. Often over time the same long term effects as a botox procedure can be observed – the muscles in the face become more and more accustomed to relaxing, leading to a permanent smoothness of the face.

A botox procedure sometimes has the side effects of headache and nausea. Hypnotherapy does not. In fact hypnotherapy patients usually wake up feeling more relaxed and happier than usual, which can aid a natural healthy sparkle and glow.

The hypnotic botox treatment follows a recent trend of other hypnotically produced operations. A hypnotic gastric band procedure has proved very popular and effective for weight loss. Hypnotic botox treatments look like they will prove to be equally as popular. This is not surprising as they are cheaper, have no side effects, and are as effective, sometimes more so, than the real procedure.

Author Resource:- Jon Rhodes is a popular clinical hypnotherapist from the UK. He is co creator and owner of HypnoBusters hypnosis downloads website. Please click here for details of his massively popular botox hypnosis audio session.

Fed Up With Social Anxiety Disorder?

by

Roseanna Leaton

Social anxiety Disorder has been given a lot more attention by the medical profession in the last ten years. If you suffer from it, you know what it feels like and how it affects every area of your life. It causes considerable distress and discomfort as the sufferer worries about what other people may think about them. This fear of being judged and fear of becoming embarrassed can be very debilitating.

For some this fear is only experienced in certain circumstances, with certain triggers, perhaps only when in the vicinity of "people in authority". For others it may just be certain places which act as the trigger to their inner turmoil; maybe a weekly essential visit to the supermarket or just having to walk down the street is enough to get palms sweating and heart palpitating. For some, just the thought of having to leave the house is enough to set this uncomfortable ball rolling. The myriad symptoms of social anxiety may be triggered by actual reality or just anticipation of something which may or may not happen. In either case, the symptoms experienced are equally real.

Whether the anxiety experienced is generalized or more specific it is still very uncomfortable and debilitating for the sufferer. Most people have serious difficulty in their quest to overcome it. This is not surprising because as you focus on trying to overcome social anxiety you inevitably spend more time thinking about it, and what you think about tends to become "bigger" in your mind and therefore in your life as well.

This is a central aspect of how your mind works. Think about it for a moment. If you are thinking about buying a particular car, for instance, perhaps a BMW or Lexus, you will suddenly become aware of every car that you see which fits that description. Suddenly there seem to be so many more BMW or Lexus cars on the road! Another "thing" which your mind does all of the time, without fail, is that if you try to not do something, you will have an overwhelming instinct to do exactly that which you are trying not to do. Try as hard as you can for a moment to NOT see a giraffe...What happened? Did you see a long neck, by any chance?!

Applying this to your attempt to overcome social anxiety disorder will help you to understand why the task can be so difficult. The more you think about it the more it happens, and the more you try to not think about it the more it happens as well. Added to this you probably have no idea why you "got it" in the first place. There will be a reason why. A symptom does not occur without cause, although you are most likely unaware at a conscious level of what that cause may be. Your subconscious mind will however know what the cause is and has created these patterns of behavior which you no longer wish to have.

How can you go about altering these subconscious patterns of feelings and behavior? A visit to your local analytical hypnotherapist (please check for the one with the highest level of relevant credentials and the most experienced) will show you how to relax in hypnosis, thereby accessing the workings of your inner mind, your subconscious, and then guide you to uncoil the springs of cause and effect which led to these symptoms being experienced. This will help you to understand why it all happened and will relieve a lot of the anxiety experienced.

But you are likely to still require a certain amount of mind re-training for you to feel completely comfortable in social situations. It's a bit like you know you no longer need to feel like "that"...but you don't know how you should expect to feel either. It can feel like you are in "limbo". Hypnosis downloads are amazingly effective in training your brain to expect to feel as you want to feel. They are inexpensive (a major bonus in the current environment), easy to use and quick to work. You really can learn a whole host of mental skills which will enable you to feel comfortable in every situation which you may encounter. I created my "complete confidence program" of hypnosis downloads for this very reason - to enable everyone to have access to learning all the mental skills needed to be confident in life at very little cost.

Whether you decide to visit a therapist in person or not, hypnosis downloads are a great choice for you to make to get your mind working on overcoming any type of social phobia. Hypnosis is in itself a state of relaxation providing welcome relief from anxiety and, more importantly, provides access to the subconscious mind, enabling the easy retraining of your mind to provide you with powerful inner and outer hypnosis confidence. There's a free hypnosis download which you can get from my website and try it for yourself.

Roseanna Leaton, specialist in hypnosis downloads for hypnosis confidence.

Author Resource:- With a degree in psychology and qualifications in hypnotherapy and NLP, Roseanna Leaton is one of the leading practitioners of self-improvement. You can get a free hypnosis mp3 from http://www.RoseannaLeaton.com and find how totreat depression naturally and overcome depression.

Searching For a Cure For Depression?

by

Roseanna Leaton

I was watching television the other day and was surprised by an advertisement for a supplement which was intended as an adjunct to anti-depressant drugs. I wish I had noted what was said but a statistic was stated about the number of anti-depressants which don't affect the required cure for depression. The percentage was really very high.

It is always difficult to trace the root cause of depression. Is it a chemical imbalance which results in depression, or is it a pattern of thought which results in a change in chemical balance? In reality, an interaction is constantly at play between mind and body which has a cyclical effect.

Anti-depressant drugs inevitably provide an intervention from a chemical angle, but cannot treat the way in which you think or tap into your habitual thought processes. The ideal treatment for depression would in fact include approaches from both angles. Unfortunately due to the cost of professional time, it is easier and cheaper to purely prescribe drugs to help overcome depression and overlook methods of treatment which involve modifying the way in which you think.

We all know that the way in which we think automatically triggers an emotional reaction. If you think about your favorite movie a smile will probably cross your face; it automatically lifts your mood. If you contemplate a horror movie you will associate with the heart pumping, tight chest, sitting on the edge of your chair (or head underneath a pillow!) response it elicits. Thoughts create emotions and their associated chemical effects throughout your physiology.

One aspect of depression which is extremely frustrating is the helplessness experienced; you feel out of control. It is therefore important to do everything you can to regain a sense that you are once more in the driving seat in your day to day life. Taking a tablet makes you feel that you are doing something which will hopefully cure depression, but is there not more that you could be doing as well?

The placebo response in drug trials is normally seen to be at around 30%, which tells us that just by thinking that a treatment will work places you in the position that your treatment for depression is 30% more likely to be successful. You could use hypnosis to access your subconscious mind and make suggestions to create a positive expectation of successful treatment of depression. In this way you can feel far more in control, and work on your depression from the mental perspective as well as from a chemical angle.

Hypnosis is a natural state of relaxation and you can learn to use hypnosis easily with the help of a hypnosis mp3 download. This is inexpensive (you can get a free hypnosis relaxation download from my website) and you can get started right away. With hypnosis you have easy access to your subconscious mind which is that part where habitual patterns of thought are stored. Suggestions can be made to retrain your mind to think is a different way. Remember your thoughts create your emotions and the chemical reactions which are felt within your physiology.

You can use hypnosis to regain a feeling of control, change your deep rooted patterns of thought and lift your mood.

Roseanna Leaton, specialist in hypnosis mp3 downloads for health and well-being.

Author Resource:- With a degree in psychology and qualifications in hypnotherapy and NLP, Roseanna Leaton is one of the leading practitioners of self-improvement. You can get a free hypnosis mp3 from http://www.RoseannaLeaton.com and find how totreat depression naturally and overcome depression.

Lose Weight by Savoring Delicious Food without Feeling Guilty

by

Roseanna Leaton

You want to lose weight. You need to eat and you should enjoy eating, so why feel guilty? What does guilt achieve anyway? It's not as if the guilty feelings have prevented you from eating; guilt is only experienced whilst actually eating food or after eating. Guilt achieves nothing other than making you feel bad about eating.

And surely eating something gorgeously delicious should make you feel good, not bad? After all, you eat for nourishment and when you are feeling well nourished you feel good. Enjoying good food is part of enjoying life. It should satisfy your taste buds as well as your need for nutrition.

I have heard many people comment upon how unfair it is that so many thin people seem to be able to eat food which is laden in fatty calories and yet still stay thin, whilst they themselves manage to put on weight simply by looking at a plate of lettuce leaves! But is this really the case? Can you really eat any diet which you choose without thinking about calories and still stay slim?

Yes, individuals are subject to their own metabolic differences, which are also related to the amount and types of exercise which they partake in. But metabolism is not the only reason why some people put on weight whilst others do not.

Let's examine for a moment the habits and thought processes of those people who seem to eat whatever they want without gaining weight. You will usually find that they eat relatively slowly, and savor the taste of the food which they are eating. You will also notice that they do not tend to overeat; once satisfied they stop eating. They do not suffer pangs of guilt and neither do they think that they should not eat particular types or amounts of food. Their minds are not tied up or restricted by a diet mentality.

If you consider the people who complain of putting on weight at the mere sight of food, you will usually notice that they are preoccupied with thoughts about food and ideas about what they should or should not have. They constantly feel guilty and so cannot fully enjoy the food which they should be enjoying. And herein lies one of the key issues; if you do not allow yourself to enjoy the food which you are eating, you will not feel satisfied, because satisfaction is not merely based on nutritional value alone.

To feel fully satisfied with your meals you need to savor the taste, smell and texture of the food which you are eating. You need to enjoy it and there is also evidence to support the requirement of a range of tastes within your meals. Thus if you limit yourself to a boring diet you will not feel satisfied, and if you do not allow yourself to enjoy your food, you will not feel satisfied.

And we all know what happens when you do not feel satisfied; you reach for more and more and more. Ironically, even whilst you reach for more food, because you are feeling guilty and not fully enjoying it, you do not fully appreciate what you are eating and it is easy to kid yourself into thinking that you are not actually eating very much. Your vision becomes distorted. And needless to say, until you fully recognize what is happening you are not in a position to do anything about it.

To lose weight successfully you have to get back to enjoying your food without feeling guilty, and to do this requires you to learn to think in a different way. This is why hypnosis presents us with such a successful approach to effective weight loss.

Roseanna Leaton, specialist in hypnosis mp3s to lose weight easily.

P.S. You too can think about food differently and lose weight easily; Grab a free hypnosis mp3 from my website.

Author Resource:- Grab a free hypnosis mp3 from http://www.RoseannaLeaton.com and find out how lose weight hypnosis works with this hypnosis weight loss program.

Social Phobia Demands a Lot of Effort

by

Roseanna Leaton

Sometimes there are hidden factors which prevent you from putting the effort into things which you would like. Anyone who is shy will identify with the feeling of being held back. You can put a facade upon your shyness and appear quite confident to the majority of people, most of the time, but you will tend to stay within your known limits. Your shyness can become an enormous barrier which prevents you from testing your limits and expanding.

Others may not realize that you are shy, and yet you yourself spend so much time worrying about what others will think. Others are more likely to think that you do not want to be doing such and such, that you cannot be bothered, and so on. A shy person, or someone with social phobia, can become so good at putting on their social mask that they do not realize what signals they are transmitting. Their main focus tends to be upon appearing unconcerned and relaxed; but others may simply think that you cannot be bothered.

Those who know you well will know that you are bothered, that you do care and that you really do want to step outside that barrier and expand in life. The people who are less likely to realize this are your work colleagues, who see you sitting quietly in meetings and discussions, doing your best to stay out of the limelight. But in this day and age, and in the types of office environments in which so many of us work, you have to find your voice and be heard so as to avoid being passed over.

When you are shy or socially phobic your effort is not a true portrait of yourself. At least, the effort which others see is not a true portrait. In actual fact you will be making far more effort beneath the surface than most other people; they just don't usually get to see it. To suffer from social phobia is hard work. Everything takes more effort than it would otherwise and you do not even get the credit for it.

You do not have to continue to suffer from social phobia. A phobia is not part of your genetic programming; it is something which is learned through experience and your formative younger years are usually the time when this anxiety pattern gets started. As the years go by you tend to live within this pattern and each subsequent experience merely reinforces your beliefs and expectations about being socially phobic.

With a little bit of help you can learn to alter these patterns of thought. Habitual thought processes are deep rooted, and they reside at the back of your mind, in the subconscious. With hypnosis you can access this deeper recess within your mind and learn new and empowering ways of thinking. Overcoming social phobia is a lot easier than you might think with the help of hypnosis.

Roseanna Leaton, specialist in hypnosis mp3 downloads to empower.

Author Resource:- With a degree in psychology and qualifications in hypnotherapy and NLP, Roseanna Leaton is one of the leading practitioners of self-improvement. You can get a free hypnosis mp3 from http://www.RoseannaLeaton.comand find how tobuild confidence and overcome social phobia.

How Can Hypnosis Help With Medical Conditions? - Part 1

by

Roseanna Leaton

The power of the mind over the body is undeniable. Science has for a long time now been providing proof for this fact. Patients in chronic pain can use mental exercises to reduce their perception of discomfort. People vulnerable to heart attacks can learn how to mentally slow down their heart rate, people suffering from stress can learn how to use their minds to reduce their blood pressure, women have been taught how to control pain in child birth, and even operations have been performed using hypno-anesthesia.

As well as this, no matter what supposedly incurable diseases there are, there is always somebody who has been cured of it. You may have heard of the miracle man, Morris Goodman, who crashed his airplane and was told he would be a "vegetable" for the rest of his life. He was told he would never breathe on his own without a respirator, he was told he would never walk again. As he says, the only thing he had was his mind, but as long as you have your mind you can put things together again - and this is what he did. As he began to breathe on his own again, the medical team couldn't work out how he had done it. As he walked out of the hospital, they didn't understand that either. It didn't make medical sense, but there is no denying that he healed himself through the power of the suggestions which he gave to himself. And every human being has this ability, this power, within them.

There is no doubt that the mind does indeed control the body. This idea has been known and acknowledged in all ancient cultures across the globe - Greece, China, India, Hawaii, etc. It is only in the Western world where medical research has somehow, over time, come to view the mind and body as separate entities rather than treating the whole person in a holistic manner. But there is now a return towards the acknowledgment of this mind-body connection. There is an increasing body of scientific evidence which reflects this and at the same time proves that the mind controls the body.

In the 1920's Dr Edmund Jacobson, physiologist and foremost researcher on relaxation, proved that when one has stressful anxious thoughts one cannot have relaxed muscles. More recently, Herbert Benson, medical doctor at Harvard Medical School, stated that "because of the fundamental unity of the mind and body it is impossible for one aspect to be relaxed while the other is tense".

In a meta-study on the effective use of adjunctive hypnosis with surgical patients, researchers at the Mount Sinai School of medicine in New York found that patients in hypnosis treatment groups had better clinical outcomes than 89% of patients in control groups. Not only that, they discovered that this result was irrespective of the method of hypnotic induction, be it live or recorded.

Roseanna Leaton, specialist in hypnosis mp3 downloads for health and well-being.

Author Resource:- With a degree in psychology and qualifications in hypnotherapy, NLP and sports psychology, Roseanna Leaton is one of the leading practitioners of self-improvement. You can get a free hypnosis download from http://www.RoseannaLeaton.com and peruse her extensive library of hypnosis downloads .

How Can Hypnosis Help With Medical Conditions? - Part 2

by

Roseanna Leaton

Every time you pick up a paper these days there is an article pointing out the fact that your mind and body are intrinsically linked. As Dr John Hagelin says "our body is really the product of our thoughts. We're beginning to understand in medical science the degree to which the nature of thoughts and emotions actually determines the physical substance and structure and function of our bodies". And to quote Dr John Demartini "Our physiology creates disease to give us feedback, to let us know that we have an imbalanced perspective".

Hypnosis is both normal and natural, and whilst you are in hypnosis you have access to your subconscious mind - the part which knows just what to do and how to do it, the part which acts automatically and spontaneously. Thus these special dynamics can be utilized to facilitate therapeutic intra-psychological communications. Hypnosis allows contact with your inner mind; it allows communication with your physiological functions.

As Michael Bernard Beckwith says "The question frequently asked is "when a person has manifested a disease in the body, can it be turned around through the power of right thinking?" and the answer is absolutely, yes".

It has been scientifically proven that each mental event triggers off nervous system activity which connects it to all other areas of the brain. Substantial evidence from psycho-neuro-immunology suggests that the mind and body communicate with each other in a directional flow of hormones and neurotransmitters. Thus every idea, thought and belief has a neurochemical consequence. Mental images, through your neural pathways, are able to transport messages throughout your entire organism.

This means that visualization techniques and symbolic imagery can be used to aid a return to normal healthy bodily functioning (for example, lowering your blood pressure, overcoming IBS), and also to kick start your body's natural ability to self heal. Your body is a self healing organism. If you cut yourself, that cut will heal all on its own. You have an immune system which guards against illness. Your body is in fact designed to heal itself. Your body knows how to return to a state of homeostasis.

As well as these more specific types of symbolic imagery, abstract imagery can be utilized - images to assist you in letting go of worries and tensions and gaining a feeling of lightness and brightness, well-being and harmony. Your imagination is limitless. It has no boundaries. A picture is worth a thousand words and a metaphor is worth a million. The creative use of metaphorical language is incredibly powerful.

Relaxation and hypnosis form the basis of this therapeutic process. Relaxation decreases the background noises and criticisms of the mind and allows you the ideal state within which to allow your creative mind to surface, thus enabling you to focus and have therapeutic direction. Hypnosis allows mental thoughts and images to have greater clarity and focus, and it allows feelings such as self-confidence, well-being and harmony to be more easily elicited.

Whilst in hypnosis your mind is very open to visualizations and you have the ability to create a more powerful sensory experience. The more real the experience becomes in the subconscious mind during this state, the more effect it will have upon what you wish to achieve. A thought without emotion doesn't have any effect. Emotions are what trigger the limbic system and the neurotransmitters which send messages throughout your entire body.

And so hypnosis can help with medical conditions in many different ways. Your mind does control your body and to treat medical conditions as purely physical symptoms would be to deny this very basic fact.

Roseanna Leaton, specialist in hypnosis mp3 downloads for health and well-being.

Author Resource:- With a degree in psychology and qualifications in hypnotherapy, NLP and sports psychology, Roseanna Leaton is one of the leading practitioners of self-improvement. You can get a free hypnosis download from http://www.RoseannaLeaton.com and peruse her extensive library of hypnosis downloads.

Section V

Resources

Sit vis vobiscum
"May the Force be with you" (Star Wars)

There are countless websites available with solid information about hypnosis. The problem can be sorting through it.

I have several favorites.

http://www.Hypnosis.edu is the website of the first nationally accredited college of hypnosis, the Hypnosis Motivation Institute (HMI). They have what has got to be the most comprehensive course material on hypnosis available in the United States today, and I cannot recommend their site enough.

http://www.HypnosisArticlesDirectory.com offers many of the articles you will find in this book and a couple hundred more. Many are reviews of other hypnosis books, several are extremely insightful works from hypnotists and hypnotherapists from every area of practice.

http://www.asch.net is the website of the American Society of Clinical Hypnosis, founded by Milton H. Erickson, MD, the father of modern hypnotherapy. It is, probably, the most reputable organization of hypnotherapists existent and publishes the American Journal of Clinical Hypnosis. It is *only* available, however, to medical, dental and mental health professionals, which bothers me as the number of growing practitioners who do not fall into those categories would greatly benefit from the educational resources the ASCH, as would the public in general.

http://www.ngh.net will take you to the site for the National Guild of Hypnotists (from which the state law guide at the end of the work comes). The NGH is a member based organization which provides its membership with numerous resources. Although it came under some fire for admitting a cat (Zoe), I am somehow not bothered by this. Zoe was admitted only as the result of a complex con perpetrated by a Ph.D. psychologist who appears to have thought it would be fun to add to his own credibility in the industry by discrediting anyone without advanced medical/psychological degrees. I suspect that if he puts as much imagination into his practice as he did into his fraud on member organizations he is probably a very effective hypnotherapist, but I have reviewed the advice of the Guild and what they try to promote (the ethical practice of hypnosis by lay hypnotists) and I somehow cannot fault them for falling for Dr. Eichel's fraud. I know cons better than most, and who better than someone with his credentials and experience to perpetrate this one? Who is more at fault - the perpetrator of the con, or its victim? The Guild (of which I am not a member, just a fan) does a good job and seems to be motivated to protect the public and the lay hypnotist. I have to wonder what Dr. Eichel's motivation was. He did, in writing about it on his organizations' audio file marketing site offer some solid advice, but I find it tainted by its self-serving mature. I think editorializing should not be hampered by (this is the reason to buy *my* product, not yours)[21].

---

[21] Yeah, yeah...I know, pot and kettle.

There are hundreds more good sites, I cannot begin to count them, but I caution you (here comes the pot and kettle thingy again) to beware of anything not provided by experienced hypnotists/hypnotherapists. I have written several articles (though not included in this work) about the dangers of the uneducated and inexperienced engaging in the practice of hypnosis, even among medical and mental health professionals[22], cannot be understated. Read, learn and learn more. Then take time to study and learn more. Find a good college of hypnosis, if you can. Apprentice with a good competent and well regarded practitioner if you cannot (or even if you can).

Keep studying. A regular, and understandable concern raised time and again, is that there are few true regulations and no real standards for hypnotists. So, we have to set our own, and the first, most basic one, has to be honesty with our clients. If we are going to be honest, level of experience must be shared and so that reading, experience in session with clients and course work is essential, both to the comfort level of your clients and to your goal of providing the very best care to them.

MSS

---

[22]Especially among them. My father, who had a Master's degree, was a psychiatric social worker for the VA, taught for Ohio State University and leaned from some of the best minds in psychology and medicine told me time and again that there is a tendency in advanced degree holders to believe that competency in one field of psychology/psychiatry somehow bestows competency in all of them. This tendency is dangerous enough in the treatment of patients who are fully conscious, it is downright dangerous when the client is not.

Section VI

Laws, Forms, Suggestions and More

Magnus frater spectat te
"Big Brother is watching you"

The National Guild of Hypnotists has provided the information contained on the following pages. It is well researched and while it is important to discuss legal details with a licensed attorney in the jurisdiction in which you intend to practice, I believe this to be a good basic guide to work from.

State Law and Legal Issues
2009 Edition

the National Guild of Hypnotists

Copyright © 2005-2009, The National Guild of Hypnotists, Inc. All Rights Reserved

This information is the intellectual property of the National Guild of Hypnotists. Intellectual property rights are claimed for its overall concept, synergy, look and feel. However, the National Guild of Hypnotists encourages other hypnosis organizations to distribute this information, believing this to be in the best interest of our common profession. The National Guild of Hypnotists requests only that its leadership in this matter be acknowledged.

The information presented here is the work of the Rev. C. Scot Giles, D.Min, DNGH, a member of the Advisory Board of the National Guild of Hypnotists. While every effort has been made to insure the accuracy of the information contained in this document, the information presented here is given as the opinion of the author, not of the National Guild of Hypnotists. Individuals should always check with their own legal counsel before acting on this, or any other advice.

Legal Issues

Stay Informed of the Law

As a member of the National Guild of Hypnotists you are entitled to the best information available on how to practice safely and lawfully. We have created this document to assist you in your practice of hypnotism and revise it each year. You will find information here on what the laws are in specific states that may affect your right to practice hypnotism. You will also find information on how to keep records, deal with issues concerning client confidentiality, required reporting laws, insurance, and other helpful matters. This document is intended to be read in conjunction with the Code of Ethics, Recommended Standards and Terminology of the National Guild of Hypnotists. If you have not read that document, be sure to do so. It will explain the Code of Ethics of the Guild (which you must follow) and the Recommended Standards for Practice (which we urge you to follow) and the words you should use while holding services out to the public.

The information presented here is intended to offer you more detail on some of the issues presented in the Recommended Standards, as well as other information. This document also provides you with the best information we have regarding state laws concerning hypnotism. These laws are constantly changing, so we urge you to keep in contact with the Guild for updates through your regional Chapter organization.

The Most Common Problems

Every year some hypnotists run afoul of the law. Typically, it is because they have made one or more very common mistakes. Therefore, we want to specifically point out these pitfalls to you so that you do not make them yourself.

First, be careful of the word "therapy." In many states the practice of hypnotism for therapeutic purposes is restricted to licensed healthcare professionals, and in some states "hypnotherapy" is deemed by the court to mean "psychotherapy by means of hypnosis." In those such it is unwise to call yourself a "hypnotherapist" and what you do "hypnotherapy" unless you are a licensed health care professional.

It is the explicit policy of the National Guild of Hypnotists to consider the traditional title of "hypnotist" to be an old, proud and distinguished title, and it is the title voluntarily used by many Guild officers. Many members do the same even if there is no legal reason to do so. It avoids legal entanglements with overly zealous governmental agencies and the Recommended Terminology of the National Guild of Hypnotists allows us to do everything we need to do under the "nontherapeutic" banner.

Second, be careful about your Title of Practice. The approved Titles of Practice for National Guild of Hypnotists members are those listed in our Standards. If you use any other title while holding yourself out to the public you are placing yourself outside of the Recommended Standards of the National Guild of Hypnotists.

The Guild awards specialty certifications in specific areas of hypnotic work such as forensic hypnotism, complementary medical hypnotism, clinical hypnotism and pediatric hypnotism. However, having received a specialty certification does not confer a new title of practice.

For example, a Certified Hypnotist who has received the specialty certification in complementary medical hypnotism would continue to refer to him or herself as a Consulting Hypnotist, not as a "Certified Medical Hypnotist." However, he or she could state that he or she was "certified in medical hypnotism" on his or her resume, stationary or business card. Similarly, a member who has received the specialty certification in clinical hypnotism could state that he or she held the certification, but is not authorized by the Guild to refer to him or herself as a "Certified Clinical Hypnotist."

Third, use the Client Bill of Rights. Giving each client an accurate disclosure of your training and limits of practice, known in the Guild as the "Client Bill of Rights" is central to our Standards. If you use one you provide yourself substantial protection from any claim that you have misrepresented yourself to the public. Failure to use one dramatically increases your risk. Instructions for creating a Client Bill of Rights are found in the Guild Code of Ethics, Standards and Terminology publication that can be downloaded from the Guild's web site.

Record Keeping Guidelines

Every hypnotist needs to keep some records on clients. While some argue that keeping records at all places you at risk (if they don't exist, they can't be produced in court to justify a legal action against you), this argument is mistaken. The keeping of basic professional records is regarded by the law as an obligation of practice. Your records are the only thing you will have to defend yourself if you are ever charged with hurting a client, placing another at risk or misrepresenting yourself.

Every hypnotist is free to keep his or her records in whatever format he or she feels is best. However, SOAP notes are an easy format to use to describe your client contacts and we recommend it. SOAP notes are common in most health care environments and having your records in this form will give them a professional appearance.

Using the acronym SOAP to describe the professional encounter with a client creates SOAP notes. When you write SOAP notes it is best to leave no blank lines and to make corrections only by drawing a line through the writing containing the error, so that it ca still be read later. These provisions will allow you to show that your SOAP notes were not altered "after the fact," and this could protect you in a court of law if someone claims you have amended your records.

Here is how to make SOAP notes:

- Date: You give the DATE of the encounter with your client.
- S: You report all SUBJECTIVE information here. Basically, this will be everything the client tells you. An easy way to remember how to use this section is the phrase "WHAT THEY SAID."
- O: You report all OBJECTIVE information here. Basically, you use this section to record what you observed about the client. An easy way to remember how to use this section is the phrase "WHAT I SAW."
- A: You use this section to report the APPRAISAL of the client's situation. You record here what you think is going on with your client. An easy way to remember how to use this section is the phrase "WHAT I THINK THIS MEANS."
- P: You use this section to record your PLAN for helping the client. You would record what sort of hypnotism you did, any scripts you used, suggestions given and any other recommendations you made (such as a book you recommended.) Finally, you would include what you think you may do at the client's next session. You may revise this plan when you next see the client, but having the plan listed here both reminds you of your thinking and makes it clear that there is a professional process of reflection included as a part of your care of the client. An easy way to remember how to use this section is the phrase "WHAT I DID AND PLAN TO DO."

Know the Codes

If you wish to know the precise use of terms in the psychological or medical environment, the terms are defined (and given specific code numbers) in two standard reference works. These are the Diagnostic and Statistical Manual of the American Psychiatric Association (currently in the fourth edition, text revised, and therefore often abbreviated as "DSM-IV-TR") and the International Classifications of Diseases of the World Health Organization (currently in the ninth edition and therefore often abbreviated as "ICD-9." The tenth edition is not yet the official guide for the United States). These volumes provide a coding system that allows all human problems to be classified, even sub-clinical difficulties like "caffeine-induced insomnia" or "nervousness." If you are a serious practitioner earning a living as a hypnotist, you probably will wish to own these volumes for reference. However, avoid using the terminology in your records.

Both DSM-IV-TR and ICD-9 contain codes used to describe routine human problems that are not the focus of a mental or medical disorder. These codes are called "V-Codes."

As the conditions described are not medical or psychological disorders (and therefore not officially part of the licensed professions), a hypnotist may safely use them in record keeping. Such codes are useful when corresponding with the members of other professions. The common V-Codes hypnotherapist might employ are listed below.

V61.90 Relational Problem Related to a Mental or Medical Condition
V61.20 Parent-Child Relational Problem
V61.10 Partner Relational Problem
V61.80 Sibling Relational Problem
V62.81 Relational Problem Not Otherwise Specified
V62.82 Bereavement
V62.30 Academic Problem
V62.20 Occupational Problem
V62.89 Religious or Spiritual Problem, or a Phase of Life Problem
V62.40 Acculturation Problem
V68.20 Request for Expert Advice

Both DSM-IV-TR and ICD-9 contain codes that are used for subclinical problems such as smoking (305.10) or simple obesity (278.0). While hypnotists may work with these conditions, there is debate about using the formal codes for record keeping. Technically, as these disorders are regarded as subclinical, the use of the codes by hypnotists is permissible. However, it may be wise to avoid any use of these codes in your records so that no one can ever put you on the defensive by challenging your right to work with conditions listed as disorders in the diagnostic and statistical manuals. A better solution is to use the V-Code for "expert advice" to indicate that the client sought expert training from you in using his or her own hypnotic abilities to cope with the problem indicated in parenthesis. Therefore, you might list smoking cessation hypnosis as "V68.20 (smoking)" and weight management hypnosis as "V68.20 (weight loss)."

As hypnotism is a different form of human service than psychology or medicine, unless you are licensed to practice medicine, psychology or some form of counseling, it is dangerous to use the terminology of those professions in your records. Therefore, avoid words like "depression," "anxiety," "compulsive," and "phobia." Similarly, avoid using the words "psychological," "medical," "clinical" or "counseling." As far as reasonably possible, use other descriptive language instead. We recommend you always follow the Guild's Recommended Terminology for Hypnotic Practice

Can You Take Insurance?

The quick answer to this question is that you probably cannot take insurance as payment for your hypnotism services. Nor should you want to.

Insurance companies exist to earn money for their stockholders. The only way they earn money is to sell policies and not pay claims. Therefore, they are always looking for a legal way to deny a claim against one of their policies. If you are a member of certain licensed professional groups (for example, a physician or a licensed clinical psychologist), there are state laws that say that insurance companies must pay for your work.

However, if you are a member of another profession, insurance companies probably will refuse to pay for your services. They can do this for any reason they wish. They can refuse because hypnotists do not have any sort of state license. Alternatively (as licensed counselors and marriage therapists have recently found) they can refuse even if you are licensed, if your state does not have a mandated provider law that says they have to pay.

Many policies contain a specific exclusion for hypnotism in any case, and even if the insurance company does pay, they will typically only pay a part of what they consider "customary and usual charges." However, insurance companies are unregulated in determining what is "customary and usual" and can set that at any figure they wish. Some hypnotists have discovered that insurance companies consider $25 per session to be "customary and usual" and they offer to pay 50% of that. This is why many successful therapists often refuse to work with insurance companies, even if they are mandated providers in their state.

The Guild feels you are better off if you set up your practice to work entirely outside the insurance system. There simply is no pot of gold at the end of the insurance rainbow. To do this, tell your clients that you do not bill insurance companies, and that your understanding is that most insurance companies do not reimburse for hypnotism. Then, collect your fee at the time of service by cash, check or credit card. Give your client a receipt showing the reason for the consultation, and if the client wishes to send it in to his or her insurance company, he or she may do so. However, to insure good will with clients it is always best to remember to caution the client not to expect the insurance policy to pay the claim. If the client was referred to you by a licensed health care professional and you were told the diagnosis, then you can list that diagnosis on the receipt you provide, along with the name of the referring professional who made it. Be careful you do not appear to be making a diagnosis yourself. You are not allowed to do so.

Some hypnotic practitioners have attempted to bill insurance companies by asking a referring physician to add the hypnotist's charges to the physician's superbill by using codes that are intended for use by Physical Therapists. The Guild does not endorse this practice.

Confidentiality

A common difficulty helping professionals have is understanding the importance of confidentiality and the limitations on it.

Like many persons engaged in helping others, hypnotists typically assure clients that anything said in sessions will be regarded as confidential and will not be disclosed. However, there is a fundamental difference between the kind of confidentiality you can promise as a hypnotist and the sort promised by physicians, psychologists and certain other professionals. We can promise confidentiality to a client, but we cannot often promise legal privilege, which is a more powerful sort of confidentiality.

"Basic Confidentiality" means that you do not intend to disclose information shared with you by a client. At most, this promise of confidentiality exists as a civil contract. If you break the confidentiality you have promised, you might be civilly sued for breaking an implied contract with your client. However, you would not be in violation of any law. In addition, if you are placed under oath at a legal proceeding, a judge has the right to order you to break your promise of confidentiality if the judge sees fit.

"Legal Privilege" means that you practice a profession regulated by a law which explicitly says not only that you must keep client confidences, but also that you may not be required to disclose in a court information given to you by a client. If you break confidentiality that is privileged, not only can you be civilly sued, but you have also broken the law and can be punished by the court. Further, except under very narrow circumstances, a judge may not order you to break confidentiality that is legally privileged. The law clearly recognizes privilege regarding information disclosed by a client (or patient) for physicians, lawyers, clergy and psychologists. In some states, privilege also exists for social workers, professional counselors and marriage and family therapists. Therefore it is vital that you be familiar with the laws in your state

In general, if requested by a lawyer or court to disclose any information about a client, you should consult your own lawyer and take the advice you are given. The advice to consult an attorney is good advice, because this issue can be legally confusing.

Test Question: As an example, imagine that you have been called to testify at a court proceeding. Imagine that the material does not fall under any privileged information law in your state. You have been placed under oath and a lawyer asked you to disclose information a client revealed to you believing that it would be confidential.

The promise of confidentiality you made to your client has no legal standing. The judge can order you to testify. However, if you testify without a fight, your client can civilly sue you for breach of contract. What should you do?

Answer: You should refuse to testify at first, explaining that you have given your promise that the information would not be disclosed. Then, if the judge orders you to testify, politely agree to do so, but request the judge's order in writing for your records prior to testimony. When the written order is received (or if the judge, on the record, refuses your request for a written order), you may testify. Your client might still bring a civil suit against you, but such a suit would be unlikely to succeed because you clearly attempted to honor your promise to your client. Also, be aware that it is possible to request the judge to hear your testimony "in camera," which means off the record in the judge's chambers so that the judge can make a decision whether or not your testimony is relevant to the trail. If the judge rules that your testimony is not relevant, the judge may excuse you from testifying at all.

Release of Confidential Information

From time to time the hypnotist may need to discuss a client's care with hypnotism instructors or supervisors, or other professionals. Prior to disclosing confidential information for these purposes it is wise to obtain a signed "Release of Confidential Information" from the client to insure that the client consents to your plan to discuss the client's care with a third party. You do not need to obtain a release to discuss a case with colleagues or instructors provided you do not share information that would allow your client to be identified. However, if you are discussing a person specifically by name or in a way that would allow another person to figure out whom you are speaking of, a release is needed.

There is no standard format for a "Release of Confidential Information." However, it is generally accepted that such releases should be fairly specific and time-limited. These are the formats we suggest:

The One-Way Release (Use this form if all you need to do is to transmit information to some other party. It is especially useful if the client wants you to send information to an insurance company, as it makes clear how much privacy the courts have ruled the client is giving up if the client attempts to use insurance to pay for your services.)

I hereby authorize [your name] to release to [the other professional's name, or the name of the insurance company] the following specific medical, psychological or educational information he or she may have pertaining to me: [List information to be disclosed.] I state that I have examined the records to be released and approve of this release to the party indicated above. This authorization for the release of confidential information expires ninety (90) days from the date below. I understand that I may revoke this release at any time on written notice to the parties involved, and that information released prior to the receipt of such notice is not a breach of my right to confidentiality. I understand that by authorizing the release of my records to a third party in this way I lose any right to confidentiality or privilege over my records. I understand that by authorizing the release of my records to a third party in this way I create a circumstance where [your name] might be required to enter testimony in a court of law regarding me. I understand that by authorizing the release of my records to a third party in this way I create a circumstance where [the other professional's name, or the name of the insurance company] may reveal the information contained in my records to whomever they wish. I understand that by authorizing the release of my records to a third party in this way I create a circumstance where the records released may be subpoenaed by interested parties to use as evidence in a court of law. [print client's name, attach signature and date]

The Two-Way Release (Use this form if you wish to consult with another professional or to acknowledge a referral. The client gives up much less privacy with this release as the information is passing from one confidential relationship to another. Never use this release to authorize sending information to an insurance company).

I hereby authorize [your name] and [the other professional's name] to release to each other any and/or all hypnotic, medical, psychological or educational information they may have pertaining to me.

This authorization for the release of confidential information expires ninety [90] days from the date below. I understand that I may revoke this release at any time on written notice to the parties involved, and that information released prior to the receipt of such notice is not a breach of my right to confidentiality. [print client's name, attach signature and date]

HIPAA

The U.S. government implemented the Health Insurance Portability and Accountability Act of 1996, usually called "HIPAA" or H.I.P.A.A.

You probably know about this law because every health care provider in your life started handing you a "Notice of Privacy Practices" in April 2003, and your mailbox started to fill with offers from various organizations to sign you up for a class where you could learn how to comply with HIPAA in your work as a hypnotist. Often, the solicitations came with dire warnings about huge fines if you fail to comply.

The purpose of HIPAA is to make it easier for people to carry their health insurance benefits with them from one employer to the next. It is also intended to make it easier for health care providers to work with people who have different sorts of insurance policies by standardizing how records are kept, transmitted and used. Finally, it intends to give the public a measure of protection over who can know private medical information about them.

Corporations and practitioners who are governed by HIPAA are required to disclose to every client what can and cannot be done with private health care information (that is why you have been receiving that "Notice of Privacy Practices"). They are required to have in place a system of business policies that meet common-sense requirements about privacy protection both for paper records and for electronic records. The requirements are basic considerations such as a rule that files are to be kept in secure locations, staff are to be trained in privacy practices, every office is to have a "Privacy Officer" and an "Electronic Security Officer" who insures compliance, etc.

Generally speaking, Consulting Hypnotists who are not also practicing some other regulated profession are not obligated to comply with HIPAA. HIPAA applies to regulated health care professionals and health care corporations. Under the laws of most states hypnotists are not considered health care professionals. If you called someone in your state government to ask if you must comply with HIPAA and they said "yes," it is likely the person you were speaking to mistakenly believed that hypnotists are regulated health care professionals under the laws of your state.

Some hypnotists are actually dual professionals possessing credentials both as professional hypnotists and in some other form of regulated health care. People such as this are regulated under HIPAA because of their second credential, and should have received information from the appropriate agency about how to comply long before HIPAA was implemented.

However, the wording of HIPAA does contain some ambiguity, which is typical of a huge piece of omnibus legislation such as this. This ambiguity does create problems for hypnotists.

For example, in Indiana, hypnotists are regulated by a committee that is part of the medical board of the Indiana government. This probably does not make hypnotists health care professionals for the purposes of HIPAA as the hypnotist regulatory act does not say that they are. But at some point or other this could be re-interpreted.

Similarly, hypnotists in Washington and Colorado are regulated as "unlicensed" psychotherapists or counselors. Does this mean they need to comply with HIPAA? It's not clear. And those states with Health Freedom Laws, such as Minnesota, Rhode Island, California, etc., where hypnotists are authorized to practice "Complementary" medicine are a real muddle. There is no authoritative answer, and it's not clear what governmental body has the authority to give an answer.

In those states where the application of HIPAA to hypnotists is unclear, the individual practitioner must decide how he or she wants to proceed. The Guild can't make an unconditional recommendation as the Guild is not a governmental agency and would be liable for any advice we give. If we said you should comply and it turns out that you don't have to, we could be sued for putting you through considerable inconvenience. If we said you don't have to comply and a court later decides that you do, we'd be liable for having given incorrect information. Because the law is ambiguous and because the Guild does not have the authority to decide this on its own, it's up to you.

Fortunately, there is nothing in HIPAA that says you can't comply with it on a voluntary basis. Therefore, the safest counsel if you are in an "unclear" state, or just want to do what other professionals are doing, is to comply on a voluntary basis even if it turns out you do not have to. It's not really all that hard and there are many books you can obtain that will explain how to comply if you choose to do so.

STATE LAWS

Current Information as of July 2009
(Updates posted in the Legislation Section of the NGH Member On-Line Forum)

Unregulated States (19 states)

To the best of our knowledge, the following states have no regulation that affects hypnotism:

Alabama, Delaware, Georgia, Iowa, Kansas, Kentucky, Louisiana, Maine, Massachusetts, Michigan, Nebraska, North Dakota, Oklahoma, Oregon, Pennsylvania, South Dakota, Vermont, Virginia, and Wisconsin.

The Guild recommends you follow Guild Standards and Terminology in these states even though there may not be a legal requirement to do so.

Guild Standard States (15 states plus District of Columbia and Ontario)

We are aware of one or more laws currently on the books that could be interpreted to prohibit a Guild hypnotist who is not otherwise qualified to practice some other profession, from practicing hypnotism. In many cases this prohibition on hypnotism is indirect—the law was not created to ban hypnotism and our concern is only about how some of the language could be interpreted. It is our opinion that you may practice in these states within Guild Standards provided you identify yourself as a "Hypnotist," call the service you render "nontherapeutic hypnotism," use only approved Guild Terminology and add to your Client Bill of Rights the following paragraph:

"The services I render are held out to the public as nontherapeutic hypnotism, defined as the use of hypnosis to inculcate positive thinking and the capacity for self-hypnosis. I do not represent my services as any form of health care or psychotherapy, and despite research to the contrary, by law I may make no health benefit claims for my services."

Alaska, Arkansas, Arizona, District of Columbia, Hawaii, Maryland, Mississippi, Missouri, Montana, New York, Ohio, South Carolina, Tennessee, Texas, West Virginia, Wyoming and Ontario.

Regulated States (16 states)

There is an explicit law in these states that regulates the practice of hypnotism. In order to practice lawfully in these states you must comply with the law. Contact the Guild office or your Chapter organization for specific details on how to comply. In all cases you must follow the Recommended Standards. In most cases there is more that you have to do.

California, Colorado, Connecticut, Florida, Idaho, Illinois, Indiana, Minnesota, New Jersey, New Hampshire (regulation voluntary, otherwise Guild Standard), New Mexico, Nevada (forensic hypnosis only), North Carolina, Rhode Island, Utah, and Washington.

Andrew Bexson

> *Common Questions Asked About Hypnotherapy* 18

Michelle Chapple

> *Stress and Hypnotherapy* 63

Rachel Ford

> *Can Hypnosis Really Help?* 16

Scot Giles, D.Min.

> *State Law and Legal Issues* 88

Evian Gillette

> *6 Actions to End Food Cravings Using NLP* 38

Jonathan Groves

> *How To Hypnotize Anyone Through The Power Of Suggestion* 15
> *Persuasion Techniques--Hypnotic Language Declined* 28

Alistair Horscroft

> *Do You Listen or Do You Hear?* 41

Orik Ibad[23]

> *Main Hypnotic Suggestions You Should Use In Hypnosis* 24
> *How Can You Hypnotize Someone Instantly?* 26

John Koenig

> *How to Declare Your Independence from Addictions Using Hypnosis* 54

---

[23] This has got to be a pseudonym.

Bryan Knight

    Hypnosis to Heal Male Rage 57

Roseanna Leaton

    Can Everyone Be Hypnotized? 13
    Fed Up With Social Anxiety Disorder? 73
    Searching For a Cure For Depression? 75
    Lose Weight by Savoring Delicious Food without Feeling Guilty 77
    Social Phobia Demands a Lot of Effort 79
    How Can Hypnosis Help With Medical Conditions? - Part 1 80
    How Can Hypnosis Help With Medical Conditions? - Part 2 81

Brenda Matthews

    What to Expect During a Hypnotherapy Session 62

Jimmy McIntyre

    How To Effectively Use Tag Questions in Hypnosis 20
    Hypnotic Language: How To Easily Embed Commands 22

Geraldine Paynter

    The Making of an Effective Anchor 34

Sue Preston

    A Gut Feeling - IBS & Hypnotherapy 53

Jack Rhodes

    The Life Altering Power of Hypnosis 11
    Get Beautiful Skin With Hypnosis 69

Jon Rhodes

    Article Submissions For Hypnosis Sites 50
    Hypnosis And The Fear Of Crowds 67
    Get Beautiful Skin With Hypnosis 71

Linda Simmons

    The Telephone Session 29

Linda Slater

    NLP Anchoring – How to Overcome Cravings and Bad Habits 32

Michael S. Spillan

    Treating Your Tools with Respect or Everything I Ever Needed to Know About Hypnosis I Learned in High School 3

    Hypnosis - Focus and Memory A New Approach To Healing 5

    Online and Telephone Hypnotherapy - Successfully Helping Clients Remotely 44

Nathan Thomas

    The Handshake Interrupt And Pull Instant Hypnotic Induction 9

Andrew Willie

    5 Simple Ways to Use Video in Your Hypnosis Business 48
    Why Every Hypnotist Must Have a Web Site 49

I would like to thank all of the authors whose articles and summaries appear in this work. Please, continue writing and sharing your experiences, in doing so you bless us all. MSS